D1301212

Wolfgang —

I am enjoying this book!

It is great to see the history arranged
& discussed so well!

Ride Free always.

Willie G.

Harley-Davidson
Photographic History

To Wolfgang
with all my best &
my appreciation for producing
an outstanding book on
Harley-Davidson -
Vaughan Beals

Harley-Davidson Photographic History

Archive, Racing, Folklore

Wolfgang Wiesner

Printed in
Hong Kong

Motorbooks International
Publishers & Wholesalers Inc
Osceola, Wisconsin 54020, USA ®

This English language edition first published in 1989
by Motorbooks International Publishers & Wholesalers Inc, P O Box 2, 729 Prospect Avenue, Osceola,
WI 54020 USA

© English language text Motorbooks International
Publishers & Wholesalers Inc

First published in 1987 by Motorbuch Verlag, PO
Box 1370, 7000 Stuttgart 1, West Germany

A department of the Buch- und Verlagshaus Paul
Pietsch

©Motorbuch Verlag

First published in 1989 by Motorbooks International
Publishers & Wholesalers Inc, P O Box 2, 729
Prospect Avenue, Osceola, WI 54020 USA

© Wolfgang Wiesner, 1989

All rights reserved. With the exception of quoting
brief passages for the purposes of review no part of
this publication may be reproduced without prior
written permission from the publisher

Motorbooks International is a certified trademark,
registered with the United States Patent Office

Printed and bound in Hong Kong

The information in this book is true and complete to
the best of our knowledge. All recommendations are
made without any guarantee on the part of the
author or publisher, who also disclaim any liability
incurred in connection with the use of this data or
specific details

We recognize that some words, model names and
designations, for example, mentioned herein are the
property of the trademark holder. We use them for
identification purposes only. This is not an official
publication

Library of Congress Cataloging-in-Publication Data
Wiesner, Wolfgang
    [Harley-Davidson, im Bild. English]
    Harley-Davidson, a photographic history / Wolfgang
  Wiesner.
    Translation of: Harley-Davidson, im Bild.
    ISBN 0-87938-343-7 (pbk.)
    1. Harley-Davidson motorcycle—History 2. Harley-
Davidson motorcycle—Pictorial works. I. Title
TL448.H3W5413   88-37576
629.2'275—dc19   CIP

On the cover: Harley-Davidson Super Glide, right,
and Fat Bob. *Harley-Davidson Motor Company*
On the back cover: Elvis Presley aboard his Harley
in 1956. *The Enthusiast*

Motorbooks International books are also available
at discounts in bulk quantity for industrial or sales-
promotional use. For details write to Special Sales
Manager at the Publisher's address

Contents

Dedication

To the lunatics, scattered all across the globe, who chase after decrepit parts, send hundreds of letters, run up huge long-distance bills, rummage around in foul-smelling crates at swap meets, go into paroxysms of delight over rusty junk for which they then pay absurd prices and shed tears over tattered brochures so that they may, after thousands of hours of hard work, again move obsolete motorcycles under their own power, even though faster and much more modern designs are available.

Acknowledgments

Normally I don't read acknowledgments. But I beg you to recognize the following lovers and collectors of American motorcycles. In supplying this book with their knowledge or background, they have overlooked or tolerated many of my human frailties.

I would particularly like to thank Buzz Buzzelli and Steve Piehl, responsible for public relations at the Harley-Davidson Motor Company, Inc., in Milwaukee, Wisconsin, who managed to straighten out my chaotic style of work; Wolfgang Hubner, factory endorsed mechanic, who tried to convey some of his four decades of experience with Harleys; Achim von Barnekow, genial collector, whose archives of literature and ideas were of great help; Benito Battilani, president of the Italian vintage motorcycle association, for his flawless early racing Harleys and much more; Bud Ekins, former racer, stuntman and at present TV and motion picture outfitter, who has preserved in his heart and his workshop the pioneering days of American motorcycles; Mike Parti, multiple sidecar Grand National champion, former club biker and now restorer, who still preserves a little-known tradition; Ray Borges and others at the archives of Harrah's Automobile Collection; Joe Koller, perfectionist and enthusiastic motorcycle historian; my honored colleague Dr. Helmut Krackowizer, for whose archival materials, photos and advice I am most grateful; Bruce Chubbuck from Harley-Davidson's West Coast fleet centers; Markus Wehner of the German *Easyriders;* and Carlo Heller, master of engineering and expert on pre-World War I motorcycles. I also wish to thank Steve Wright, as well as Mike Shundo, Gregory Walter and *Easyriders* publisher Joe Teresi along with Hans Weschta and Klaus Zobel. But most of all I'm indebted to Willie G. Davidson, who let me in at all!

Christel and I visited them and many others. Thanks to them, our lives in this past year have been more interesting and colorful. But not only their machines impressed and delighted us, several have since graced us with the pleasure of their friendship.

For this we are most grateful.

Preface

Harley-Davidson contracted out most historical photos to Pohlmann Studios or purchased them from independent photographers in order to complete the company archives and to permit their use in company publications. The expense of maintaining an in-house photo lab or even full-time photographers, historians and the like, who could have spent decades on endless journeys to cover just the national racing scene, was simply too high for the always financially strapped managers of the relatively small company.

Pohlmann Studios not only has an illogical, undated cataloging system, but also lacks any listing of available pictures. In the company archives, few photos are identified by so much as a name or year. Buzz Buzzelli claims that those responsible are aware of the situation. After 1980, however, the first order of Harley-Davidson business was mere survival; contemplation of the company history was far less vital. Half of the staff, including the archivist, became victims of that fight for survival. When this book reaches print, there will probably again be a historian on staff. It will take years to examine, catalog, evaluate and absorb the material on hand. But someday, in perhaps five or six years, friends of the Harley-Davidson tradition will again have a clear, bubbling fountain of facts at their disposal.

To correctly organize the data in this book, I have done research at the plant, auditioned American and European collectors and colleagues, dug into many unfamiliar collections and in the process have gone through mountains of American motorcycle magazines, *Enthusiasts* and other company literature, and diverse American publications on the Harley-Davidson story. Should the observant and knowledgeable reader find faults (he who is totally free of fault is to be envied), then I beg him not to cast the first stone but rather to address me by writing the publisher.

This volume will certainly appeal most to enthusiasts because Harley-Davidson is printed on the covers, which in turn display high-quality original factory photos. My commentary and explanations as well as the color photos hopefully will be gladly accepted and induce the undecided buyer to purchase. But the fact is that this book, although in part mine, is really a Harley book.

Wolfgang Wiesner

February 1986. Christel and me at Joe Koller's in Wisconsin, on his unrestored 1916 rig.

Chapter 1

Early days

In 1901, Fred Merkel of Milwaukee presented his first "motor cycle" in an attractive little brochure. It was a bicycle with a motor mounted above the pedal crank bearing, with the exhaust fed directly into the frame. Whether this actually reduced noise, no one can say, as the first Merkel bike no longer exists. Certainly, the frame was not strengthened by the holes drilled into it, nor was it any cooler due to the exhaust gases fired into it. Regardless, Merkel sold several of them, because after all, what else could his customers buy? Neither the market for nor the selection of such devices were highly developed.

Those who wished to propel a motorized two-wheeler had a choice of several unfinished designs. This may have been the final shove that, in 1901, induced Bill Harley and Arthur Davidson, two young metalworkers who had been friends since childhood, to concern themselves over how a small engine, moreover a complete motorcycle, should appear and function. Arthur's brothers Walter and William, also metalworkers interested in all things mechanical, became increasingly involved with their experiments. These four, after several setbacks, soon developed their first motorcycle, surprisingly modern yet robust. In the magazines of 1903, only the Werner cycle comes to mind as a similarly innovative design.

In all likelihood, the four founders, in their limited spare time, built only one cycle in 1903, three in 1904 and five in 1905. With the money remaining from early orders, they purchased tools and hired their first employees. With these first co-workers, they produced fifty examples of this type in 1906. Early customers were won over by the comparatively modern design, the heavy flywheel and low center of gravity in a motor mounted in a sturdy single-loop frame, governable via spark and carburetion, the tightenable belt drive and the care in material selection and design.

The advertised performance of the first Harley-Davidsons was impressive and may be considered not far removed from reality; otherwise, word of mouth among enthusiasts quickly would have stifled further development of the young plant. A top speed of 45 mph was claimed, and the tank capacity of 1.5 gallons was said to be adequate for a minimum of 100 miles. The two quarts of oil were allegedly sufficient for 750 miles. A gallon of gasoline cost about ten to fifteen cents. The problem was finding it; the first gas station was not opened until 1912, in Los Angeles.

Of the company founders, Walter Davidson was particularly active in testing prototypes. His technical feel was matched by his riding skill, as proven by his competition successes. Arthur Davidson, during his long rides to win over new agents across the land, gained firsthand experience with the new motorcycle. Bill Harley was equally renowned as a "motorcycle nut"; when he, as the responsible designer, was not found working with his tools or on components for the machines, he was most likely testing them outside. He often took his older and more sedate friend, William Davidson, on rides in sidecars; of the four, Bill Davidson was the only one who didn't particularly relish riding the new invention. Regardless, it was his job to convert the changes engineered by the other three into pro-

duction, without halting work or releasing new products before they could be properly developed.

This connection with practical experience was the basis for the healthy, pragmatic, humble and realistic outlook of the firm's founders. As a result, they seldom had reservations about using components supplied by others, if it was felt they were better or more economical than what they themselves could make. Although at that time Colonel Bowden was still demanding high license fees for the use of his patented cables, the men behind Harley-Davidson chose to use these serviceable components, rather than the expensive and temperamental (but free) rods and universal joints employed by other makers. Similarly, Harley-Davidson used Bosch magnetos for

The first motorcycle to carry the Harley-Davidson name.

many years, rather than the less expensive and less reliable domestic product.

On the other hand, they were eager to surpass the quality of bought-in parts. Their own electrical system, which eventually replaced the magneto, was superior to its predecessor. Their own sidecar could easily withstand comparison with the outside-supplied product once distributed by Harley-Davidson. After some difficulty, they even produced their own bolts.

The company's principle was to offer proven, reliable designs, even if it meant losing the race to market to more impetuous firms. This was first shown with the sound development of the springer fork. This classic design would hold sway for the next forty years, with occasional updating and improvements. George Brough, heedless of any expense for his Brough Superiors, bought into the spring fork license for use on his peerless product, and used it for twenty years.

According to a brochure of 1913, the plant area grew in size from 200 square feet in 1905 to 200,000 square feet in 1912, the work force grew from four to 1,076, and production went from five to over 17,000 motorcycles. The rapid growth continued almost up to the Great Depression which began in the late 1920s. The first Harley-Davidson building then found a place of honor in the later company property on Milwaukee's Juneau Avenue. Plant visitors were gladly received there. This continued until World War II, when an outside contractor mistakenly bulldozed the shed to make room for yet another plant expansion. It seems he took it to be merely an outdated shed, which, in a way, it was.

From old Harley-Davidson ads, a visibly proud Walter Davidson, posing for the early sales materials, looks back at the reader. His

The Harley-Davidson plant, after it doubled in size. William C. Davidson, father of the three Davidson brothers, was a carpenter and cabinetmaker and *built a shed in 1903 on the family property to house his sons' hobbies; in 1905 it doubled to the size shown here.*

15

self-esteem was well founded. With efforts toward sleeker styling, a higher self-assuredness on the part of the four founders became apparent after about 1911. Harley-Davidson introduced countless solutions to problems faced by the young industry. The Ful-Floteing saddle, introduced in 1912, was kept for decades. Two adjustable progressive springs located in the seat post, totaling about fourteen inches in length, supported the seat pin. Thus the saddle had about four inches of vertical travel, in addi-

In the midst of the Juneau Avenue plant, the first Harley-Davidson building found a place of honor, until it was mistakenly torn down. One fewer attraction to show the welcome visitors.

tion to the inch or so allowed by the springs on the seat mattress.

The unsprung frame was retained, because other clever suspension concepts, such as the cantilever by Merkel or leaf springing as used in Indians, were still plagued by rear wheel wobble. Considering the condition of the roads at that time, the Ful-Floteing principle offered an improvement in comfort. The 1912 model came with a further advance, the Free Wheel Control developed by Bill Harley and his co-worker Henry Melk. Installed in the rear hub, it made getting under way easier and may safely be regarded as the first motorcycle clutch.

In the summer of 1913, Jack Purdy and Harvey Bernard motivated their sidecar across the trackless prairie and equally trackless, but even more grueling Rocky Mountains, from Chicago to Denver by way of Cheyenne, Wyoming. Motorcycle journals of the day were glad to report news of this sort, in order to point out the totally hopeless condition of the road system of that time. In the fall of 1912, for example, the first sidecar tour from New York to Chicago was completed. The first stop sign in the United States was installed at a Detroit intersection and exhorted motorists to drive carefully. In 1914, Cleveland installed the first green, yellow and red signal, vanguard of the countless traffic lights now seen the world over.

Also in 1914, the V-twin showed many improvements. The rear hub-mounted two-speed transmission and the clutch were not the only advances, however. The step starter markedly eased start-up of the chain-drive models; no longer did the bike have to be started while on its stand. For pedaling, the new footboards could be flipped up. The Harley-Davidson band brake was a sophisticated in-house development, which turned out to be more expensive than the bought-in components used previously. The new system was double acting, with expanding shoes inside the drum and an external band around it. The clutch could now be actuated by foot as well as by hand.

The top model for 1915 was equipped with yet another new transmission, the three-speed, destined to remain for many years, situated in

The factory still on the Davidson's property on the corner of 38th Street and Highland Avenue, the family home in the background. The inset shows the backyard shed where it all began.

its now familiar location. Also new were improved bearings and a simpler but sufficient oil pump.

Because Harleys were finding increasing use with officialdom, particularly the postal service and police, large corporations and, after 1916, the US Army, local dealers were overwhelmed with service and repair demands. Also, the technology of the machines was becoming more demanding. An unskilled tinkerer wouldn't

17

Walter Davidson, spring 1906, astride a prototype showing a development version of Bill Harley's springer fork arrangement which did not go into production. In the background at left is the burgeoning plant, at the right the Davidson family house. Note the unpaved road, common at that time.

find much success working on Harleys. As a result, the Harley-Davidson Service School was founded in 1916, offering courses lasting several weeks; the school exists to this day.

The efforts of the factory for American defense were recognized by the War Department with the usual honors, such as a huge flag. The US military alone possessed 15,500 solo and sidecar Harleys by the end of the First World War. In addition, virtually all Allied forces in Europe put imported Harleys into front-line service. The larger displacement and robust design philosophy showed itself superior to the economy-minded design of European motorcycles, particularly on the long supply routes and bottomless mud of the battlefields of France and Flanders.

After the war, the 1000 cc machines were well known in all Allied countries. They were, however, never sold in great numbers, because

In 1907, 154 machines were delivered. From then on the springer fork, developed by Bill Harley, was installed. This was considerably stronger and more robust than the one shown earlier. It soon was regarded as the standard of the industry, and in comfort and wheel control was superior to such devices as the front leaf springs as used by Indian. Otherwise, this single cylinder still shows exposed control cables and battery ignition.

In 1908, 35 workers built 450 Harleys. The cylinder was cast without lower cooling fins because Bill Harley intended to put magneto ignition in front of the similar forward cylinder of his V-twin, then still under development, and no other location could be found. The fork was somewhat straightened and the second container added between rear wheel and frame. The function of the belt tensioning and release mechanism is visible.

In 1909, displacement was increased to 35 ci, 500 cc, the flywheel was enlarged, the single cylinder was again cast in a different form and the exhaust port was not as far to the side. The control cables for ignition and throttle were routed within the handlebars, and those parts remaining outside were covered with leather. Battery ignition was retained on the single.

19

the import duties for European countries and their colonies resulted in high prices, with which no great market penetration could be achieved. Furthermore, in Europe the larger displacement bikes incurred higher taxes and insurance premiums.

In the United States, motorcycles were arranged in power classes for taxation and insurance. Consequently, the power ratings in historical documents do not correspond with actual engine output. For example, a 61 ci twin was rated at 8.68 hp for several decades, while a 74 ci twin was taxed at the rate for 9.5 hp. The plant advertised most as 8 or 9 hp models. Everyone knew what was meant. Top speed claims,

rare at that time, tell us more about the power output. At the time, American motorcycles were considered especially powerful, fast, innovative and robust when compared to their European contemporaries.

The British motorcycling press tested a big Harley every year; as early as 1918, they found the power output to be about 18 hp, although the plant maintained its far lower claim. In reality, the inlet-over-exhaust big twins of the 1920s easily put out triple their 8 or 9 hp rating. When power or speed claims in the contemporary motorcycle press are compared, great differences are often apparent and are difficult to reconcile today.

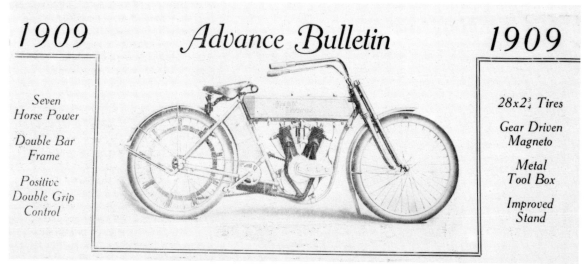

Bill Harley's first V-twin was almost production ready prior to 1908. This early version was announced as the Model 5D in a premature bulletin for

1909. Fuel was supplied by a high-mounted Harley-Davidson carburetor; drive was by cog belt.

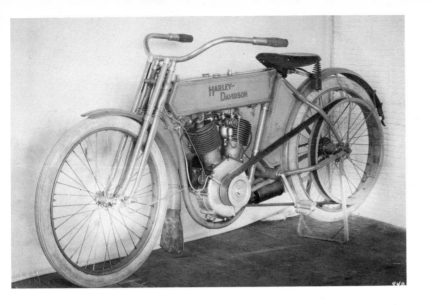

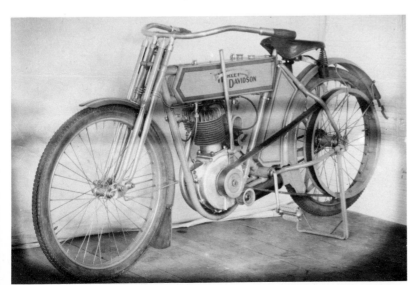

When the Harley-Davidson V-twin reached the market in 1909, it was equipped with the smaller 1908 cylinders, no longer used elsewhere. As there is no tensioning arrangement for the belt, the question remains of how belt slip was controlled; some kind of hand clutch was probably used. At the front of the motor is the gear-driven Bosch magneto. Instead of a Harley-Davidson carburetor, a Schebler unit was used, which was cheaper because it was built in great numbers. Displacement was 49.48 ci, 800 cc. The bike had no transmission, and in spite of the well-known Harley-Davidson workmanship, neither the buying public nor the plant were particularly sad to see it go in 1910, not the least because the "automatic" suction inlet valves were obsolete. At the time, it did not appear to be a great leap forward. Today, the first Harley-Davidson twin would be the high point of any collection.

The single-cylinder of 1910, with Mabon clutch on the handgrip and cog belt. For a while, Harley equipped its machines with V-belts, but soon discontinued this practice. This photo, along with those of the other machines taken in this corner, were not commissioned by the company until much later (sometime in the 1920s). The bikes were dredged out of the cellar. The fate of this machine is unknown, as it is neither in the Harley-Davidson museum nor in the associated storeroom. No further information is available, but the bike may be experimental, as indicated by the guide for the clutch lever remaining on the tank.

From 1911 onward, Harley-Davidson motors were equipped with mechanically driven inlet valves, which gave an immediate power increase and a more pleasing appearance.

21

William A. Davidson, Walter Davidson, Arthur Davidson and William S. Harley; photographed prior to the First World War.

*The Ful-Floteing seat as well
as Free Wheel Control were
introduced in 1912. Free
Wheel Control was one of the
first functioning motorcycle
clutches.*

*For model year 1913, the
optional chain drive could be
ordered to replace the
obsolescent leather belt.*

One of these two probably had to walk home, unless the pilot was somehow able to set the young lady on the tank, without interference from the long clutch lever or still longer handlebars.

In the summer of 1913, Harley-Davidson public relations man Frank Rodgers called attention to a new development of Bill Harley's: the Motorcycle Truck. A prototype was satisfactorily put into service in the winter of 1912–13 by the US Post Office for parcel service in Milwaukee. Offsetting the purchase price of $425 were operating costs of three-quarters of a cent per mile. The soon-beloved trike-truck was considered maneuverable and easy to handle. The two-speed transmission, installed first on the truck, used ratios of 5:1 in high and 10:1 in low gear, and fit the temperament of the chassis well. The factory quoted a maximum cargo capacity of 550 lb., although many less considerate teamsters were known to load up to half a ton.

A V-twin of 1914 with two-speed transmission installed in the rear hub, tank-mounted shift lever, clutch action via hand lever or foot pedal, step starter, new footboards, and band brake. This couple has equipped their 1000 cc Harley for touring, with a sidecar by the Rogers Company of Chicago, costing $75, freight not included. Also note the Prest-O-Lite acetylene lamp, with tank mounted on the rear frame, the speedometer drive from the front hub and the air pump on the fork.

Harley-Davidson

Pour tous les sports

Model 11-J, the 61 ci V-twin, was the top model for 1915. It was equipped with a new three-speed transmission, located in the right place, which was to remain in service for many years; improved bearings; a simpler but totally adequate oil pump; and about 30 percent more power. The lighting was sophisticated, part of the combined ignition and lighting system by Remy. The front lamp had two bulbs; the rear lamp could easily be removed and used as a work light. The factory also included an electric horn, luggage rack and trunk-mounted tool kit in the package. The frame was lowered slightly, resulting in the hemispherical indentations in the fuel tank. The price of the Model J was $310, significantly higher than other Harleys of that year. Of course, twins or singles with one or two gears and without the Remy equipment could be had more reasonably, at prices starting at $200 for the single.

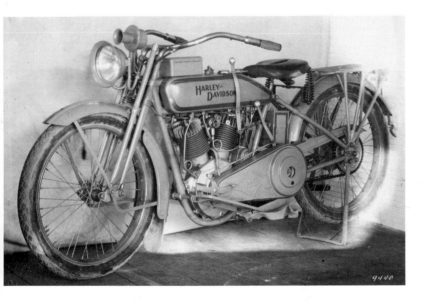

From 1917 to 1922, Harley-Davidson marketed their own brand of bicycles, built in cooperation with the Davis Sewing Company. Nine distinct types are known. In addition to this racing model and Joe Koller's example, shown in the color section, dealers could order diverse heavy or lightweight touring models, ladies' and children's bikes. Due to less than overwhelming sales, the founders finally realized that motorcycles and bicycles appealed to two distinctly different markets. That meant that the reputation would again have to be built up in the new market, a course which understandably was not taken.

27

Government offices, police departments, the US Mail, private companies and, after 1916, the US Army put tens of thousands of Harleys to work. Many unknowing mechanics had to maintain them. For them, a course of instruction lasting several weeks was developed. The Harley-Davidson Service School was founded in 1916, and exists to this day.

Changing shifts meet at the front entrance, sometime during World War I. The War Department commended the plant for its dependable deliveries by bestowing its Excellence Award and other associated honors, such as the large flag.

Early single 17C of 1917. To reduce manufacturing costs, after 1916 the plant simply installed the single-cylinder engine in the twin's frame. The tank for the Model C was unique; it had only one indentation to clear the single rocker arm of its one and only exhaust valve. The lack of an additional cylinder is quite noticeable. At a price of $240, the C was $30 to $70 less than the J and F twins. Because of war production and public demand as well as the plant's desire to concentrate on twins, manufacture of single-cylinder models was halted in 1918.

In the middle of model year 1917, the factory replaced its familiar gray lacquer of ten years with military olive. Even the crankcase was so-colored in heat-resistant paint. This was not done, as the advertisements would have us believe, in sympathy for the boys Over There. Rather, the countless motorcycles and sidecars ordered by the military had to be delivered in this color, and it only made sense to deliver civilian machines with the same treatment rather than set up a separate paint process. Little changed for 1918. The plant was operating at full capacity.

A 1918 Army model with Prest-O-Lite illumination.

The factory grounds on Juneau Avenue, undergoing yet another expansion in 1919. During the first 20 years, departments had to move regularly, and often had to work under makeshift conditions. Often, production was running on the ground floor while the walls of the second floor were still being installed.

Chapter 2

The Wrecking Crew

Before America's entry into World War I, there were recurring disagreements over promotion of races, safety regulations and licensing in professional as well as amateur racing among the organizers, industry, press, the Federation of American Motorcyclists (FAM), the first national motorcycle organization, and then internally among committees and leadership of the FAM. Interest in the popular events on the part of the leading motorcycle manufacturers waned.

Walter Davidson was particularly fond of competition and, in 1905, was successful as the first factory rider. Often the lead was contested by competing teams staffed by Bill Harley, Arthur Davidson and their clever employee Lacy Crolius, later to be in charge of advertising.

Avoidable but often deadly spills were almost routine on the steeply banked board tracks, rarer on the flat and dirt tracks, and the oil-soaked horse racing tracks. The immediate consequence was always quick placement of blame and cries of "I told you so." After a severe accident claimed the lives of seven at the new board track at Newark, New Jersey, on September 8, 1912, the then-dominant firms of Indian, Excelsior and Thor officially withdrew from racing until mid-1913.

Relations among the manufacturers were not always cordial. In June of 1912, for example, a four-valve Indian works machine was stolen from the paddock of the Philadelphia motodrome. On pure suspicion, without a shred of evidence, Indian, in the following weeks, accused a competing firm of organizing the theft in order to learn the secrets of the Indian's speed and dominance.

The sport continued without company support. At the end of 1912, two Harley-Davidson riders, unsupported by the company, set a new flat-track record of 350 miles in seven hours. In the summer of 1913, privateer riders at the infamous and important 225 mile road race from Harrisburg, Pennsylvania, to Philadelphia took the first three places in both the one- and two-cylinder classes. Other successes soon followed. Lacy Crolius, the shrewd Harley-Davidson advertising man, ran full-page ads in the fall 1913 issues of *Pacific Motorcyclist*, *Motorcycling* and other journals to the effect that, although the factory in no way supported racing activities, Harleys were winning more races than ever. The *Silent Gray Fellows* from Milwaukee were

This 30.50 ci racer of 1914 is the first fruit of the cooperative efforts of William Harley and William Ottaway, soon to dominate the American motorcycle racing scene; it was usually raced on short quarter- or half-mile dirt tracks. The front cylinder of the more modern V-twin engine was equipped with a heavy flywheel and mounted on the crankcase of the 5-35 single-cylinder. Inside, they worked carefully and conservatively. They lightened and polished all moving parts, installed special pistons, enlarged the carefully fit inlet valves and equipped them with stiffer springs, and raised the rev limit, compression and power output by use of an easily adjustable carburetor and hemispherical combustion chamber. The wheelbase of the normal Harley-Davidson was considerably shortened. The nonspringing racing fork and auxiliary manual oil pump on the tank are notable. Full development of the racing one- and two-cylinders was to take a while longer. It was not until 1916 that Harley-Davidson was the team to beat.

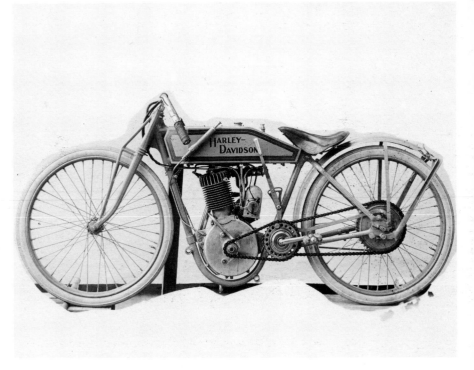

not only reliable, as was well known, but also quick.

At this time, such encouraging results caused a small racing department, attached to the design department, to be founded. To staff it, William Harley lured the well-known racing director and designer, William Ottaway, away from Thor in Chicago. Ottaway had worked for Thor's parent company, Aurora, from 1895 to 1913. Among other things, he was said to have been part of the team that designed the long-lived one-cylinder motors built by many Aurora licensees, including, from 1901, Indian. It was the fast, white Big Valve Thor racers that paved the way for his position at Harley-Davidson. In December of 1913, he took on his new job as Harley's second designer and first tuner.

In the first months of the racing department's existence, the factory engaged interested dealers in the organization and financing of the new racing team. On July 4, 1914, the annual 300 mile race at Dodge City, Kansas, took place. It was considered an ultimate test of the machines' endurance, an "Indianapolis for motorcycles." The press as well as the public paid particular attention to this race. Only two of the six Harleys entered reached the finish line, one forty miles off the pace, the other over sixty miles behind the winner. Still, at the 120 mile mark, a Harley rider was dueling for the lead with the eventual winner, on an Indian, before dropping out with chain and ignition problems. William Harley and William Davidson, attending the race, had seen enough. Had their racers been better prepared, they could have held their own against the eight-valve Indians. Back in Milwaukee, the four founders resolved to carry out their racing efforts more thoroughly.

Before becoming a Harley rider, Maldwyn Jones dominated the half-mile tracks with a Merkel which he modified himself. In 42 starts, he won 24 races, finished second ten times and third three times. In the remaining five races, he was involved in spills or had mechanical problems. He is said to have invented the steel shoes used by dirt-track racers; he was certainly the first to use them with virtuosity in his riding style. In all, he raced for Flying Merkel for six years, before that company's demise in 1916. Jones had had friendly contacts with Bill Ottaway for some time, and was a welcome addition to the Harley-Davidson team from 1916 onward. After tests with works machines, Jones retained Merkel frames and forks for his short-track efforts. The interesting-appearing four-valve motor was a new eight-valve job, minus the front cylinder. Jones stayed with Harley until 1921. In 1922 he went to Excelsior as a professional rider, and later worked as manager of the carburetor manufacturer Schebler, supplying almost all of the industry at that time.

34

In September 1915, at the 100 mile event marking the opening of the spacious Maywood Board Speedway near Chicago, the Harley-Davidson works riders, on their Ottaway-tuned pocket-valve racers, nearly shut out the opposition. The average speed was 89.11 mph, a new world's record. These machines were thence-forth feared as "Chicago Harleys." At the left, in the infield, the team pits. The Chicago wood track was relatively long and did not possess the raised, banked (up to 60 degrees) turns of the quarter-mile "soup bowls" being erected across the land by promoter Jack Prince.

On November 26, 1914, the official Harley-Davidson factory team entered the 300 mile championship race at Savannah, Georgia, for the first time. There were multiple retirements due to spark plug problems, but the best-placed Harley-Davidson rider, Janke, finished third.

Increasingly, Bill Ottaway was becoming the key figure in the efforts of the works team. He applied his talents as tuner, selected drivers in his capacity as racing chief and gave his crew disciplinary direction. His riders had to train regularly, learn to adjust themselves to their teammates during a race, maintain physical fitness and comport themselves before a race in a decent if not restrained manner. No driver was favored by the choice of machine or by team orders, a policy which maintained the competitive spirit within the team.

As his experience increased, Ottaway surprised the opposition with tactically sound race preparation, which made for close, time-saving cooperation between pilots and well-trained pit crews. Even with routine operations like refueling or tire changes, the Harley team saved many seconds, if not minutes, over their rivals.

In the 300 mile championship race in Savannah at the beginning of 1915, Janke on a Harley again finished third, behind an Indian and an Excelsior, but among the first eight finishers were four Harley pilots, making for the best team finish. Otto Walker and Red Parkhurst soon garnered a one–two finish in the important 300 miler at Venice, California.

Walker also won the July 4, 1915, 300 mile event at Dodge City, Kansas, in a new record time. Except for an Excelsior rider in third place, the first seven finishing slots were filled by the team from Milwaukee. All eight Harleys finished, six of them beat the previous year's record time; all in all, a striking and much discussed victory. From that date onward, Ottaway's rid-

Red Parkhurst's race against an airplane, around a dirt track. Such half-time spectacles were beloved by spectators as well as professionals. One group loved it for the variety, the other for the added income. No doubt fun was had by all; Parkhurst naturally won.

36

ers were to win the important 300 miles of Dodge City until the event ceased, after World War I.

Ottaway was decisive in the organization behind these sporting successes. The brand name Harley-Davidson owes much of its early national fame to him. Floyd Clymer, another impressive early pioneer of American motorcycle history, served as a works rider for Excelsior, Indian and later, Harley-Davidson. He recalled that Ottaway introduced the team's brilliant yellow or orange and black sweaters, and insisted on their being worn—not because of their adver-

tising value, but so that during a dusty race he could identify his drivers from the pits and have flag or pit board signals ready.

During 100, 200 and 300 mile races, the riders had to circle the one- or two-mile courses more than a hundred times. They were unable to tell their own position or that of their competitors. They also could not tell precisely when they were due in for refueling or tire changes. Ottaway kept them informed with pit boards and directed his team from the pits with pre-arranged flag signals. By means of hand signals, drivers transmitted their wishes or problems to a trackside observer long before they reached the pits; the observer would telephone the information ahead.

Although racing stables were maintained by Cyclone, Emblem, Merkel, Pope and Thor, the marques Indian and Excelsior remained Harley-Davidson's targets, Harley's goal was to undermine their superiority on the track as well as in the marketplace by winning races to boost the image and provide advertising fodder. The Wigwam's racing department offered their riders not only 30.50 ci intake-over-exhaust (ioe) singles developed by Hedstrom but also a like-sized four-valve single and a 61 ci twin with eight valves. They remained the fastest in their class for a considerable time. After 1915, the avant-garde Cyclone overhead-cam racers were passing all of the other works teams, but these fragile yellow machines seldom reached the end of a long race.

In 1915, Harley and Ottaway decided to develop a pushrod eight-valve based on the pocket-valve engine. In contrast to the cylinder head of the Indian, with its four upright valves per cylinder, they opted to angle the valves at 45 degrees, and thus were able to increase the valve area, create a hemispherical combustion chamber, use domed pistons and increase the compression ratio appreciably, resulting in a power increase.

For the 1916 Dodge City race, Ottaway put a new eight-valve engine at Clymer's disposal. In practice, he blew away everything else on the track, but had problems with a lean mixture, which he attributed to the high temperature.

UNDER THE RULES AND DIRECTION OF THE FEDERATION OF AMERICAN MOTORCYCLISTS.

Price 10 Cts.

EVERY SATURDAY AND SUNDAY—RACES BEGIN 3 P. M.

OFFICIAL PROGRAM
SUNDAY, AUGUST 11th
VAILSBURG STADIUM MOTORDROME

Eastern Motor Racing Association

GEO. W. CROSS, Pres.
PAUL J. C. DERKUM, Mgr.

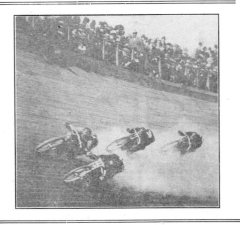

38

At the 200 mile championship event at the Ascot Speedway near Los Angeles in June 1919, Harley riders filled the first five places, against well-staffed teams from Indian and Excelsior. First across the line was Ralph Hepburn, followed by Parkhurst and Weishaar. Several generations of spectators at the still-functioning Ascot Park were to witness countless Harley-Davidson victories at the dirt track.

Bill Ottaway, right, and Hank Syvertsen, left, had put together a team that was to be not only hellishly fast but also had good camaraderie. There is no information available on this photo, but judging from sweaters, tent and faces, I would guess it was taken in 1917. From the left: Hank Syvertsen, Fred Ludlow, Maldwyn Jones, Ralph Hepburn, Ray Weishaar, Red Parkhurst, Otto Walker, Jim Davis, and at the far right, Bill Ottaway.

In February 1920, at Daytona Beach, Parkhurst, right, and Frank Ludlow, left, established several world records recognized by the European FIM. Parkhurst on the solo eight-valve covered the flying mile at 112.61 mph. The sidecar reached 83.9 mph over five miles. In the back, one of the timers; R. Enos, a manager for the Harley racing team; and Hap Scherer, from the advertising department and long-time editor of the Enthusiast.

Rather than attack the problem by enriching the mixture (and thereby losing power), he rigged a wind deflector which was later adopted by the Harley racing department and also the competition. In the race, while contesting the lead with Janke, Clymer suffered a burst tire at 100 mph. Somehow he got back to the pits, took on fuel and tires, proceeded to repeatedly break the lap record, and was again leading at 218 miles when a broken valve put him out for good. Janke, on the other eight-valve Harley, won the race, three miles ahead of Wolter on his racing Excelsior. Weishaar, on an ioe Harley, was a distant third ahead of two eight-valve Indians.

The Harley-Davidson works team avoided the board tracks, concentrating on noteworthy long-distance events, which it often won against bitter resistance from the other teams. Thanks to these exciting events, the sport gained popularity. At the Phoenix 200 miler, the 150 miles of Oklahoma City or the 100 miles of Chicago, practically anywhere they raced Harley-Davidson riders set new records and humbled many an opponent. The records for five, ten, twenty and fifty miles, too, fell to Harleys.

At the insistence of the FAM, the firm was forced to offer its eight-valve engines to privateers. With incredibly high prices of $1,500 for

40

Ray Weishaar brought a piglet into the team as the Wrecking Crew's mascot. Perhaps the Harley nickname Hog has its origins here?

In any case, the piglet was dressed in its own Harley-Davidson team outfit and apparently enjoyed being served Coca-Cola by Ray Weishaar. This scene is from Marion, Indiana, 1920. Weishaar won many a race for the team until his untimely death in a race at Ascot. These photos were left to the company by works rider Ray Weishaar.

Efficient cooperation with suppliers, such as Firestone, was important; parts and accessory manufacturers made maximum use of this in their advertising. At the bottom right, the team hog. The rider here was Brownie Carslane.

41

the twin and $1,400 for the single, private buyers were probably effectively locked out of the market. It was different with the pocket-valve production racers, fast machines in their own right. In 1915, for example, these sold for a more bearable $250. In addition, the works assisted less-well-known riders with bonuses and special parts who, on any weekend, contested the countless events on flat tracks, board tracks, hillclimbs and enduros from coast to coast. Talented and ambitious local heroes were supported by dealers and were regarded as a pool of future talent.

As it became apparent that the United States would enter the Great War, the motorcycle manufacturers agreed among themselves to halt their racing activities in order to concentrate on government contracts. In 1917 and 1918, racing was supported solely by dealers.

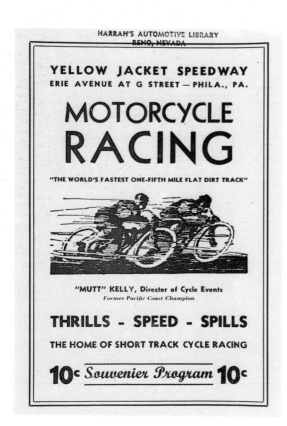

HARRAH'S AUTOMOTIVE LIBRARY
RENO, NEVADA

YELLOW JACKET SPEEDWAY
ERIE AVENUE AT G STREET — PHILA., PA.

MOTORCYCLE RACING

"THE WORLD'S FASTEST ONE-FIFTH MILE FLAT DIRT TRACK"

"MUTT" KELLY, Director of Cycle Events
Former Pacific Coast Champion

THRILLS - SPEED - SPILLS

THE HOME OF SHORT TRACK CYCLE RACING

10c Souvenir Program 10c

After the war, the FAM, the first motorcycle organization in the United States, finally folded, thanks to internal dissent, lack of any viable concepts and general lack of interest. The manufacturers enlarged their own industrial league, the Motorcycle and Allied Trades Association (MATA), which altered the sporting regulations beginning in 1919. Wooden tracks under one mile in length were outlawed. Dangerous, oil-spewing ports in the cylinder heads were also banned. Only 30.50 ci machines were allowed to race on half-mile flat tracks. As of 1919, the factory racing teams of the reduced number of manufacturers returned to the racetracks. Again, Harley-Davidson garnered the lion's share of victories, ironically including the trophy sponsored by the Indian works.

The Riders Division of MATA, founded in 1920, organized sporting events beginning in 1921. In 1924, it was spun off from the parent organization and continued under the name of American Motorcycle Association (AMA). The AMA remains the supreme American motorcycle sanctioning body.

The professional Harley-Davidson racing team, the Wrecking Crew, as well as several other Harley-Davidson pilots won every national championship in 1921. The years of growing dominance were royally crowned. When one thought of speed and motorcycles, one thought of Harley-Davidson. What a moment to choose to officially leave the sport!

Walter Davidson let it be known that the factory had, for some time, been divided into two distinctly separate businesses. One was the continually growing racing department, with its salaried riders, designers, mechanics and office staff, which had to prepare and participate in each important national race. That side of the business brought a great deal of fame and recognition, but at a high cost in wages, expenses, engineering talent and preparation. As a result, these funds were lacking in the other side of the business, the manufacture and sale of motorcycles. Bill Harley added that there were more designers occupied in the racing department than in the normal engineering department: that situation could not continue. As of

Marion, 1920. The riders used celluloid or wire screens to protect their eyes, and Harley-Davidson pilots wore padded gloves. Ottaway instructed his riders to maintain a sensible and constant pace and not to be provoked by competitors into machine-killing full-throttle duels. Indian rider Shrimp Burns scorched into the lead, and stayed there until his chain broke. Weishaar on a Harley then led, until Burns, making up ten to 15 seconds per lap, closed in. Weishaar obeyed pit signals and held back; soon Burns' replacement chain broke, destroyed his fuel feed and retired him for good. Weishaar, on a sturdy ioe machine, motored home to win. After the race, the new head of Indian, Frank Weschler, congratulated the also-present Bill Harley and Arthur Davidson. Harley admitted that he knew Weishaar's machine was by far not the fastest, but that he had counted on his rider's steady and considerate style, bet a few dollars and won still more.

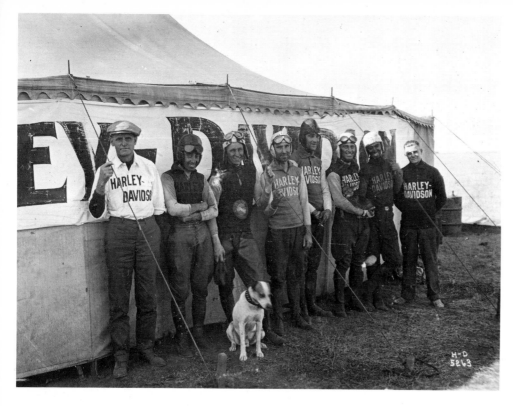

The glorious Wrecking Crew in front of the Harley-Davidson team tent, Dodge City, Kansas, 1920. From the left: racing manager Bill Ottaway, Maldwyn Jones, Ralph Hepburn, an unknown mutt, Frank Ludlow, Otto Walker, Ray Weishaar with yet another nameless mutt, Jim Davis and Hank Syvertsen, later to succeed Ottaway as racing boss after the latter became chief designer upon the death of Bill Harley. The Fourth of July fell on a Sunday, and due to local blue laws, the race had to be held on the following day. Indian, Excelsior and Harley-Davidson all sent their first-string riders and machines. During the long race on the short two-mile course, Jim Davis and Maldwyn Jones, both on Harleys, had a stubborn fight for the lead, during which Jones set new 100 and 200 mile records—until retiring with spark plug problems at 250 miles. Davis won on his ioe Harley-Davidson racer, Walker on an eight-valve Indian was second, Weishaar on a Harley was third.

Walter Davidson and William Harley, second and third from right, apparently had a good reason to be happy at this visit to an unidentified flat track in the 1920s.

1922, Harley built a limited number of racing machines and sold them to established riders, but completely withdrew its entire works racing effort.

The same was true for bicycles; the Davis company, in conjunction with the Harley-Davidson dealers, took over their support and maintenance for several years. Further work for other companies, too, was canceled. The plant was streamlined, unneeded machinery sold, rented buildings vacated and the widened Juneau Avenue used as effectively as possible.

The professional Class A battles, once contested by the works with such innovation, quieted down. For three years, Indian bedecked itself with the greatest number of laurel wreaths.

Inlet-over-exhaust 61 ci racer, vintage 1920, with, among other things, keystone frame open at the bottom, unsprung racing fork, open exhausts, clutch and band brake in the rear hub. Ottaway usually left the choice of faster eight-valve or more robust ioe engines to his riders.

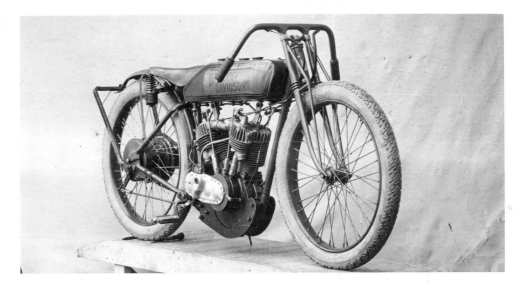

The single-cylinder, one-speed racing Model S for quarter- or half-mile tracks, 1922. The somewhat short-appearing cylinder is mounted on a V-twin crankcase; the air filter can be opened or closed for starting. The keystone frame is identical to that of the racing twin.

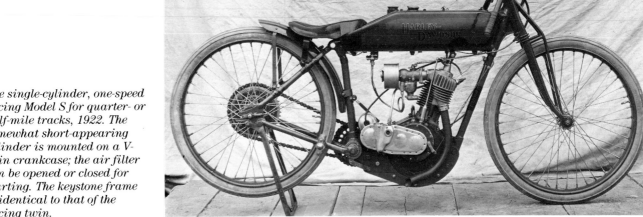

American racer Freddy Dixon emigrated to Great Britain, where, in the twenties, he won countless races on Harleys as well as Indians. He was particularly successful on the classic Brooklands track. There, on September 9, 1923, he set a new world's record for the flying kilometer at 106.8 mph, using an eight-valve Harley-Davidson. Of interest in this photo is the box surrounding the carburetor and Dixon's replacement of the open Harley keystone frame with a loop frame.

Bill Minnick, multiple sidecar champion, with a two-cam racer and flexible (hence the name FLXI) sidecar. These FLXIs, sprung within their mainframe tube, leaned with the machine in turns and could be driven almost like a solo bike up to the point of no return, at which the sidecar would lift off the ground. At this point the rider would plant his right boot against the sidecar. From that point onward, the entire rig, leaned far over, would behave like a conventional bike with an unsprung sidecar, with drifting, steering by throttle and so forth. I can imagine how claustrophobic the sidecar passenger must have felt, as the driver would get closer and closer in right turns, but be virtually invisible in left turns, except for his boot which would be aimed straight at the sidecar rider's face. It would appear that Minnick was not overjoyed with the stability of this arrangement, as he has mounted fork parts from an Excelsior for reinforcement. The front fork's friction plate is surmounted by his mascot, Felix the Cat.

In Europe, too, the rapid Yanks were successful on many courses. The scene is the Tilburg circuit,

Netherlands, 1921. Herkuleijns (at right) won the race.

Bill Minnick, in 1925, won the last board-track sidecar title with his two cam FLXI combination. In the same year, the rapidly climbing Joe Petrali and his Harley-Davidson pocket-valve racer garnered the 100 mile board-track record at 100.35 mph. Again, nine of the fourteen titles went to Milwaukee.

Beginning in 1926, privateers aboard Harley-Davidson's light, quick, sturdy 350 cc singles,

the Peashooters, won many dirt-track titles with these new production racers from Milwaukee. Hillclimbs, too, went to the small, high-revving Peashooters. As of 1928 or 1929, fast and interesting 750 cc ohvs were produced and did well at hillclimbs, even alongside the huge 1340 cc pocket-valve monsters. It was not until 1934, with the introduction of Class C, that the sport had a formula more appealing to amateurs and the remaining manufacturers.

Claude Ceresole of Bern, Switzerland, gained the Swiss 1000 cc title in 1924, 1925, 1927 and 1929. Here, at the important 1929 Guggensbach-Guggisberg race, he set the fastest time of the day despite a broken valve spring.

An early single of 1907, the first year of Harley's front fork. Is it looking back at its past, or from the past into our present? No matter; we brought this machine back to York with great care.

The first Harley-Davidson V-twin of 1909, in the York, Pennsylvania, museum, still breathes through suction-operated inlet valves. As there is no tensioning arrangement for the drive belt, you have to wonder how belt slip was tamed. Perhaps this was only a prototype and the production models had a more controllable toothed belt.

Carlo Heller of Wiesbaden, West Germany, astride his Model 6B, with 500 cc displacement, battery ignition and 28 inch tires. The Silent Grey Fellow of 1910 was no first-kicker, not the least because the pedals weren't kicked but rather turned. Regardless, the motor, maintained in original condition, fires up readily. Heller is counting the days to the next London-Brighton run for pre-WWI vehicles and hopes it won't rain.

Two jewels from Joe Koller's collection near Milwaukee, Wisconsin, whose articles in Antique Motorcycle are a treasure-trove of information. A Harley-Davidson bicycle, built from 1917 to 1922, like all Harleys from 1917 in olive camouflage. The civilian in the back is a 5-35, also known as a Silent Grey Fellow, of 1912 or 1913.

Restorer Mike Parti, hopelessly in love with early American bikes, and his 1916 rig. In the right window of his small museum in Sun Valley, California, near Los Angeles, is a comprehensive spark plug collection.

The paths on Joe Koller's Wisconsin property were still not free of snow on this mild March day, but the roads were clear. Three of us rode through hill and dale in his 1916 vintage 61 ci twin with a sidecar and were amazed at how well it pulled. Joe's rig has been kept in original condition, except for the troublesome Presto–O–Lite illumination, in whose tank Koller placed a propane gas bottle.

51

The cover of the 1917 Harley catalog provides some idea of how cross-country roads looked at the time. Motorcycles were uniformly olive-colored.

Bud Ekins of North Hollywood, California, with his Model 18C, a three-speed, single-cylinder 500 cc with magneto ignition. In 1918, the factory ceased production of the ioe singles.

Until his death, this picture of an early dirt-track racing scene hung in the office of former racer and later publisher Floyd Clymer. His widow presented it to Bud Ekins for his veteran motorcycle shop. In the fifties and sixties, Ekins won great endurance runs, for example the Baja 1000 and, as US team captain, the International Six Days Trial. His friend, actor Steve McQueen, was a member of the victorious team. At the insistence of the latter's insurers, Ekins did most of the stunts in McQueen's films.

In the treasure-trove of Imola, Italy. Benito Battilani is particularly proud of this jewel; it's the eight-valve racing machine with which Eduardo Winkler won several Italian road races and became heavyweight champion of his country. Every year, Battilani and his friends ride this as well as other early Harleys at the Italian Veteran Grand Prix in Imola.

Most competitors probably had this view of the incredibly fast and reliable eight-valves. The factory sold only a limited number of eight-valve bikes overseas, with keystone racing frame and three-speed transmission.

The author of American Racer, Stephen Wright, worked as Steve McQueen's restorer for seven years. McQueen had him recast the cylinders of this transmissionless eight-valve board-track racer. Even the experienced foundrymen of General Motors needed one year before they were able to cast acceptable cylinders capable of taking the stresses of an operating engine. The achievements of early Harley-Davidson designers and craftsmen still command respect today.

An ioe 61 ci production racer in European road-racing trim with loop frame. Viva Battilani!

Steve McQueen's early JD rig. McQueen was particularly interested in early Harleys. Other collectors felt that he ruined the market, because he would buy models he really wanted regardless of cost.

A cop probably mounted on a low-compression 1928 JDXL police bike, reproduced by Hubley in cast iron. From the collection of Horst Schallert of Berlin, dealer and collector of toy motorcycles.

Harley-Davidson's last ioe engine, the 1200 cc JDH of 1928 with the two-cam engine, strongly influenced by racing practice. Precisely because of its antiquated and, for most manufacturers, abandoned ioe design, which was developed to the fullest by Bill Harley and Bill Ottaway, this marks a high point of American motorcycle design. From the Mike Egan collection, Santa Paula, California.

The 500 cc side-valve Model C replaced the 350 cc ohv B and BA models in 1930. The latter had been particularly popular export models since 1926. Production of the C ceased in 1934. Also restored by Benito Battilani.

Paul Weyres of Aachen, West Germany, was the only person to ever be German sidecar champion for three consecutive years, 1931 through 1933, and was also successful at other European events. Alois Drax of Munich, riding Harley-Davidsons, was multiple champion in the heavy solo class.

Weyres later converted his eight-valve for street use, and, equipped with registration plates, rode his racing machine on the street, which says something about the durability of the competition motors from Milwaukee.

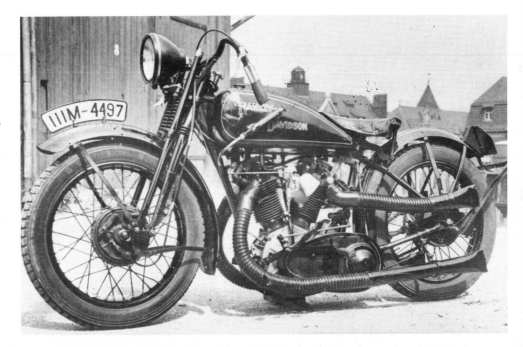

A 1929 Enthusiast, closely followed by its (former) rider, Ben Burnham, at a hillclimb near San Diego, California. Despite his two-cam ioe motor, he didn't reach the top and had to walk the rest of the way, if not push. In many publications the rider is listed as Dud Perkins. Of note in this as well as the two following photos are their differing engine and frame configurations.

SOUVENIR PROGRAM

TRAFFIC OFFICERS BENEFIT

HILL CLIMB

AL BLASINGAME HILL ON TOLL HOUSE ROAD AT HUMPHREY STATION

SUNDAY april 10

FRESNO CALIF

Windy Lindstrom was long a member of the hillclimb elite and won several 45 and 61 ci championships.

In his first year of professional racing, Russell "Kid" Fischer was national hillclimb champ in the 61 ci class. He won the title in the final event at Keck's Farm, near Rochester, New York, with a one-foot lead over old pro Windy Lindstrom. Legend has it that Kid, ever image conscious, kept an unlit stogie clenched between his teeth even during races.

Possibly a road racer for Europe or Japan; Steve Wright, author of American Racer, *believes it was a prototype for an ohv 750 street bike based on the side-valve motor. The surviving 750 cc motors were then often entered in US hillclimbs. The holes under the cylinder head were for squirting in fuel before start-up. The plant assures me that this prototype machine was built in 1930; hard times prevented full production of this promising model.*

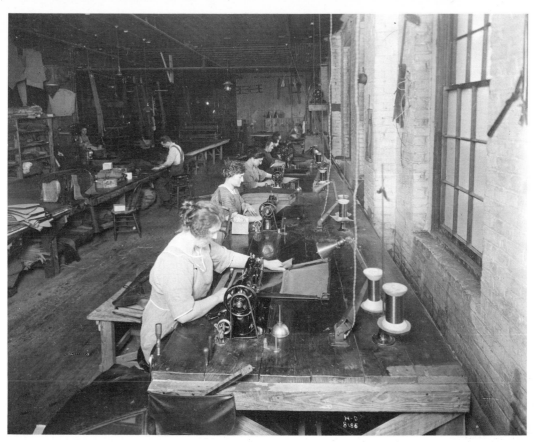

In and around the plant

The following photos of everyday life in the plant were taken after the end of the First World War and into the 1920s.

Seamstresses sewed the cut-out pieces together; in the background is the cutting table.

Covers for saddles and sidecar seats were cut to pattern on this huge cutting table.

Frame manufacturing on the sixth floor of the Juneau Avenue factory.

What a tiny paint can for so many sidecar frames!

Between coats, the surface was hand-sanded. Paint work as well as general workmanship was of a high standard and labor intensive, before as well as after the war. Mike Parti, well-known Californian restorer, and his partner in paint, Mike Shundo, have restored several sidecars from this time period, and are bemused by the careless, low-grade work on most of today's brands. Most novices, on seeing for example a 1916 sidecar rig refinished to original standard, feel it must have been over-restored.

Frame and fork testing rig in February 1921. At the front, the frame of a sport model is being put to the test. The cast-iron bedplate serves as the anchor. The torture devices are driven by Harley-Davidson motors and transmissions. It may look simple, but it did the job.

At Harley-Davidson, it wasn't all work. The atmosphere at the plant was, with rare exception, considered outstanding. Employees behaved no differently 60 or 70 years ago than today's Harley workers when they meet socially.

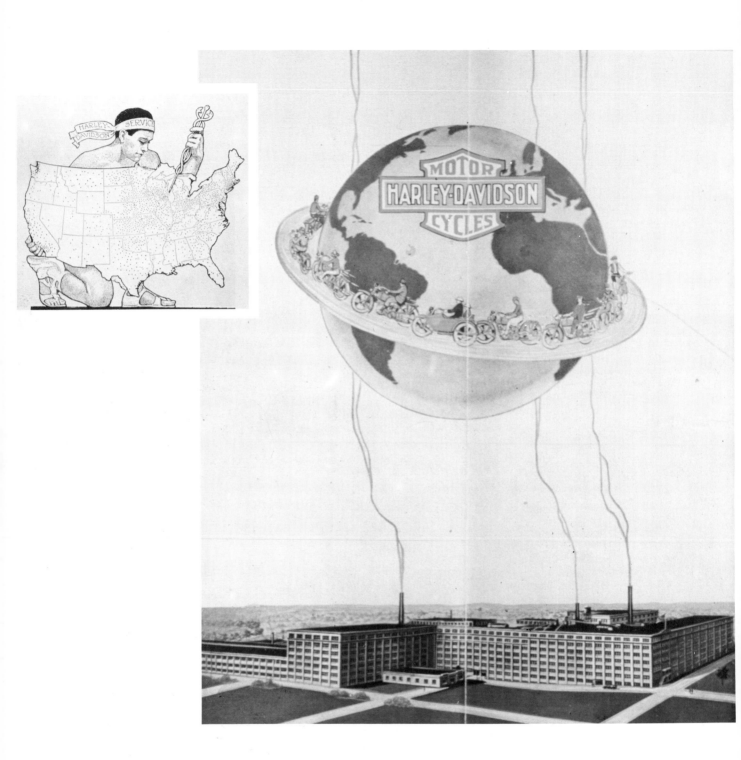

Chapter 3

The F-head era and early singles

During World War I, the development of the automobile proceeded by leaps and bounds. Henry Ford introduced the assembly line to Detroit in 1914; in 1916, the firm sold a half-million Model Ts. After the entry of the United States into the war, the front-line reports demonstrated the superior utility of the automobile compared to the motorcycle. The military establishment ordered cars, trucks and finally tanks in such huge numbers that the automotive giants, particularly Ford and General Motors, amassed vast capital, streamlined their internal processes and reduced costs to unbelievable levels. In the process, they standardized and modernized their product. After the war, the civilian market was served with even less expensive products made to a higher standard and with better materials.

At the same time, thanks to continuing full employment and high demands for labor during the armaments boom, and American exports after the war, wages were generally on the rise. Also, the new generation of entrepreneurs, who often came up from humble beginnings (Henry Ford being a prime example), practiced new, more progressive, less exploitative labor relations.

The buying habits of the American consumer also changed dramatically. The private car, which had been the privilege of the wealthy class a scant fifteen years earlier, was within tantalizing reach of farmers, white- and blue-collar workers. Its usefulness was emphasized as road building began in earnest. Car makers and banks supported the burgeoning demand for credit and deferred-payment plans. Thanks to marketing and advertising campaigns, the car gradually grew to be an important status symbol. At a typical salary of $5 a day, however, the consumers could still not afford to put a car *and* a motorcycle in the driveway. They had to make a decision, and naturally preferred the four-wheeled family and utility vehicle. Therefore, the motorcycle gained the reputation of being ridden by folks who either could not afford a car or didn't carry great responsibility.

The motorcycle industry was hard pressed to adjust to the new market situation and appeared at the end of its resources. Most of the American motorcycle marques, which once numbered nearly 200, went out of business in the 1920s at the latest. The surviving market was concentrated on the three big survivors, Harley-Davidson, Indian and Excelsior, which, thanks to their large volume, did not immediately collapse. In fact, Harley-Davidson attained record sales, with 24,000 machines sold in 1919 and 28,000 in 1920. But from 1921 onward, sales plummeted, even in Milwaukee; only 10,000 were sold in that year.

This was not changed by the impressive racing record nor spectacular successes such as that of February 1922, when Otto Walker, without factory support, attained an average speed of more than 100 mph in Fresno, California. The factory couldn't even spur sales by dropping the prices—there was no margin left. The marketing disadvantages compared to the automobile were insurmountable. In 1925, Ford offered the base Model T for under $300. Nothing could be done against that sort of competition. Harley-Davidson's sales figures represented only a fraction of those of the major car makers, which eliminated any possibility of volume discounts for raw materials or accessories. Although far fewer manufacturing steps were necessary to build a motorcycle than a car, the limited volume denied any possibility of making the required capital investments for effective assembly-line production.

Regardless, the four Harley-Davidson founders invested a large part of their accumulated capital in automating and reducing costs of manufacturing. In addition, they suffered from the tougher competition of the twenties, which required a strong development effort to have

Harley-Davidson's first side-valve, the light, popular sports model of 1919, eclipsed similar longitudinally opposed machines from Indian, Douglas and the predecessors of BMW. But at the beginning of the 1920s, when Indian's sales hit, the V-twin Scout appeared and the concept of the Sport could make no headway. Production was halted, but remaining stocks or a small special series were sold to Europe. In the home market, the factory concentrated on the big twin market and development of the ioe V-twins.

Bill Harley in the boat, and Walter Davidson at the helm, pose in front of the plant for the Enthusiast.

Postage stamp from the 1940s, showing a special-delivery courier with his 1922 Harley, representing the legendary reliability and speed of the early Harley ioe bikes.

The results of a spring weekend. William S. Harley and William A. Davidson were known for their joint hunting and fishing expeditions. This photo prompts the question, where did they stow their catch on the return journey from lake or stream? Moreover, how did they keep their suits so clean? Perhaps they just dressed up for the photographer.

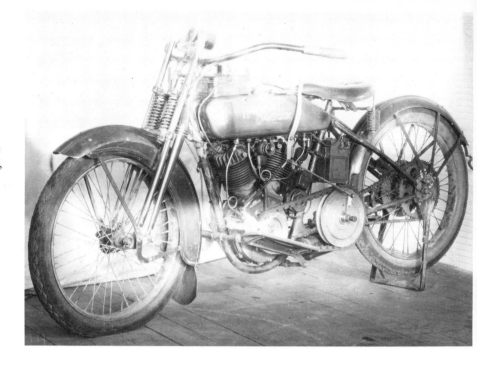

An experimental machine of 1923-24, with primary drive by toothed belt, a so-called magneto clutch with an interesting-appearing release mechanism, and a reinforced, lengthened front fork.

William Ottaway astride a 1924 V-twin. Born in New York in 1871, he entered a machinist's apprenticeship after finishing school, worked for a railroad, and moved to Chicago in 1893, where he found employment with the Aurora Automatic Machinery Company—Thor. Floyd Clymer reports that even then he had contacts with the then-inexperienced future founders of Harley-Davidson. Ottaway was later renown for his extremely fast White Thors. In 1913, the Harley-Davidson managers hired him as assistant designer and racing director. He supposedly continued to work for Harley-Davidson until after World War II, and after Bill Harley's death served as his successor in the role of chief designer. After entering retirement, he continued with consulting assignments for the company. On December 27, 1952, he transferred, as the obituary in Cycle *puts it, to that Golden Speedway up there.*

new hardware to attract a smaller part of a tiring market.

First, the company brought out the low, light and pleasant sports model of 1919, with a longitudinally installed 37 ci opposed side-valve engine, which overshadowed similar designs from Indian and European manufacturers.

In 1921, the Harley-Davidson V-twin model was powered by a 74 ci engine for the first time. This ioe Model JD was a convincing competitor to the big Indian side-valve. But the competition from the East Coast wasn't asleep, and introduced a light, fast, legendary motorcycle in the form of their Scout. The Scout attained incredible sales figures, which numbered the days of

the Harley-Davidson sports models; those responsible in Milwaukee thought the further development of the sport concept against such competition was senseless. Instead, work concentrated on the big twin, but the sport was still offered in export markets for a few more years.

Milwaukee again improved equipment as well as appearance and increased the pace of new product introductions: the much improved springer fork, standard speedometer and ammeter, Dow metal pistons, use of chrome-vanadium steels, Alemite pressure lubrication, the bent frame and the first teardrop tank, the lowered seating position for 1925 and finally, for 1926, the 21 ci single as a side-valve or ohv

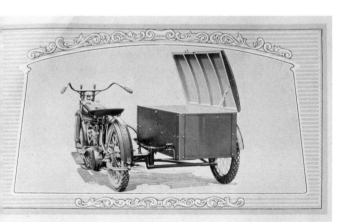

Das 1000 cbcm. Magnet-Modell mit Lieferwagen

DIE neuen Harley-Davidson Liefer-Seitenwagen zeichnen sich durch eine neue Chassis-Konstruktion aus. Das Ladegewicht ist jetzt direkt über die Hinterachse verlegt, und ruht auf zwei 40½ Zoll = 101,125 cm. langen halbelliptischen Federn. Jede Feder ist an einem Punkt der Chassis-Achse befestigt und besteht aus acht Federblättern.

Der Lieferkasten ruht auf zwei U-förmig abgebogenen Trägern, an welchen die Federn befestigt sind. Beim hinteren Träger sind für diese Befestigung Laschen vorgesehen. Diese Bauart ermöglicht, die Carrosserie den individuellen Bedürfnissen des Käufers entsprechend in verschiedenen Längen auszuführen. Der Abstand zwischen den beiden U-Seiten der Träger misst 24 Zoll = 60 cm.

Die carrosserie dieses neuen Seitenwagens behindert die Lenkung des Fahrzeuges in keiner Weise. Der Schwerpunkt der Last liegt über der Achse und der ganze Lieferwagen ist ausserordentlich leicht zu lenken. Auch hier

ist reichliche Bodenfreiheit und Abstand für eine genügende Durchfederung vorgesehen.

Der Chassis-Rahmen besteht aus kräftigem, verstärktem Stahlrohr mit starken Stahl-Stützpunkten zur Befestigung der Federn. Der Kotflügel ist auf der Achse befestigt. Sieben Alemite-Nippel sorgen für ausreichende Schmierung. Der Radstand beträgt 48 Zoll = 120 cm., die Ladefähigkeit 150-250 Kg.

Wir sind nicht in der Lage Lieferwagen-Carrosserien zu liefern, da wir solche nicht herstellen. Wir verkaufen nur das Chassis, komplett mit Kastenträger, Rad, Reifen und Kotflügel. Die für die verschiedenen Zwecke am besten geeigneten Kasten können gewöhnlich leicht an Ort und Stelle und zu einem vernünftigen Preise hergestellt werden.

Die obenstehende Abbildung zeigt eine weitverbreitete Kastenform. Für manche Geschäfte genügt ein Lieferwagen ohne Deckel. Für Schneider, Färbereien, Waschanstalten, Blumenhandlungen wird im Allgemeinen ein hoher Kasten mit senkrecht angeordneten Türen an der Rückseite vorgezogen.

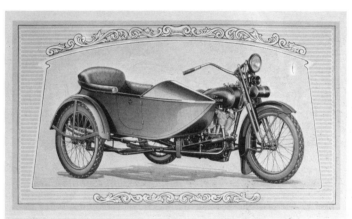

Das 1200 - cbcm. elektr. Modell mit Seitenwagen
rechts vom Fahrer

EIN Harley-Davidson-Seitenwagen verschafft Ihnen doppelten Genuss auf Ihren Motorradtouren. Wie oft haben Sie sich nicht schon gewünscht einen Begleiter mitnehmen zu können um Ihre Freuden auf den Ausflügen mit diesem teilen zu können.

Passagier und Fahrer bezeichnen ein-

stimmig den Harley-Davidson Seitenwagen als den bequemsten der bis jetzt gebaut wurde.

Die zwei 125 cm. langen halbelliptischen Federn lassen den Seitenwagen-Passagier stossfrei über Löcher und andere Unebenheiten der Strasse hinweggleiten. Verlangen Sie von Ihrem Händler eine Probefahrt, und Sie werden in Bezug auf Fahrbequemlichkeit eine angenehme Ueberraschung erleben.

Leicht einstellbare Stossfänger, hinten und vorne, absorbieren die harten Schläge und erhöhen die Bequemlichkeit des Seitenwagens für Fahrer und Passagier.

Alle Harley-Davidson Seitenwagen werden mit einer ausziehbaren Achse geliefert. Diese ermöglicht eine Erweiterung des Radstandes von 110 cm. bis zu 140 cm., einen Vorteil den jeder zu schätzen weiss der auf schlechten Strassen oder Feldwegen mit Karrengeleisen fahren muss. Die Achse ist rasch und mühelos ausgezogen wenn die Strassenverhältnisse es bedingen. Der Kotflügel folgt hierbei dem Rad, sodass der Seitenwagen-Passagier dennoch vollkommen gegen Kot— und Wasserspritzen geschützt ist.

A well-equipped F model of 1929.

engine, and improved ignition coil. In 1928 the front brake was introduced, and it was just in time, because in 1929 the JD big twins were available with the fast H-series two-cam motor.

In 1929, in the depths of the Depression, the four founders again showed their confidence in the future by first enlarging their model selection and then presenting to the public the side-valve 30.50 ci single and the four-cam 45 ci side-valve twin.

Throughout the difficult 1920s, the managers of Harley-Davidson saw their salvation in increasing specialization, and therefore made increased efforts in the commercial and service sectors, with economical alternatives to delivery

The F engine of the 1920s, with magneto ignition.

The 1927 J and JD models shone with the Harley-Davidson single-unit electrical system, which consisted of the enclosed generator mounted directly on the engine, regulator, waterproof ignition coil, six-volt battery, horn, adjustable illumination and a small control panel for ignition and lights. This replaced the bought-in, not always satisfactory Remy electrical system.

Illustrated here is a sectioned JD twin of 1924, with 1200 cc. The first motor with the legendary 74 ci was presented by the plant in 1921, and sold from 1922. As of 1924, Bill Harley strengthened the crankcase, installed aluminum pistons with improved piston rings and drilled connecting rods, and increased the number of hardened roller bearings to 36. All of that had previously been available only on racing or sports models. In Enthusiast number 63, from the end of 1923, which introduced the 1924 twins, "Hap" Hayes reported that vibrations had decreased appreciably, and that he estimated the power gain at 25 to 30 percent.

The commercial Package Trucks, the hard-working sidecar combinations with 74 ci motors, had lowered compression by means of a plate inserted between cylinder and crankcase. These models had an additional S in their serial numbers. Countless customers ordered a wide variety of sidecar styles.

One of the many commercial sidecar applications. I would venture that this may have been a rolling hot dog stand, or perhaps the owner sold roasted chestnuts or something like that. Why else would the exhaust be routed through the sidecar? In any case, business must not have been all that great, or else the owner could have afforded to replace the bald tire on the bike. Built in 1926 or 1927.

cars and trucks. For the most varied business uses, countless custom designs were made, usually based on the 74 ci units with sidecars.

Thanks to their economy, maneuverability, speed and light weight, the well-equipped solo bikes for police duty gained increasing sales. Approximately 3,000 to 4,000 police departments put Harley-Davidsons into service. The remaining two marques, Indian and Excelsior, vainly tried, without success, to gain a foothold in that market. The neatly uniformed traffic officer, usually waiting for offenders at the side of the road astride a black-and-white Harley, was a commonplace, if not exactly welcome, sight in the United States. The big Harley was—and is—the classic police bike.

For younger buyers and those interested only in economical transportation, Harley offered the smaller, low-priced 350 cc single, on sale from 1926 onward. The combustion chamber shape was licensed from Sir Harry Ricardo. Its economy and reliability of operation were especially valued in export markets.

In order to give added impulse to the increasingly vital export business, the factory supplied interested and capable foreign importers with reworked racing machines, with which their own drivers could gain victories and recognition in their national events. For certain countries, the factory provided specific versions. In Europe, the racers from Milwaukee soon gained attention in Great Britain, Germany, Italy, Sweden and Switzerland. Their pilots won countless championships in the larger classes, including sidecars. The ioe as well as the eight-valve engines achieved legendary status as fast, heavy motorcycles.

William Harley and his second-in-command William Ottaway grabbed many key words and phrases from the burgeoning auto industry. After the marketing mileage that Henry Ford made from his firm's use of chrome-vanadium steel, they examined its usefulness and soon used it for their own product.

Further, they recognized that a good part of their customers did not buy motorcycles be-cause they needed them, but rather because they were fun. The JH and JDH two-cam models, in particular, appealed to this circle of customers, the "gentleman riders," which put a high priority on power and comfort. Their motors were a bit more civilized, but optically and mechanically similar to those of the famed FH competition models. These machines were the pinnacle of eighteen years of intake-over-exhaust engine development.

SPORTS

Motor Boating   Golf   Baseball

MOTORCYCLING -
The Greatest Sport of them ALL!

Fishing   Tennis   Horse Racing

and with a Harley-Davidson you enjoy Motorcycling at its Best

Dom.   Printed in U.S.A.

The last ioe big twin of 1929, in the 74 ci two-cam version, was named JDH. The standard "flute" at the tip of the exhaust allegedly produced less racket without appreciable power loss, and presumably was intended to look good. The front brake was standard from 1928 onward. On the higher-end models, speedometer and luggage rack were included.

The two-cam FH motor, famed on track and hillclimb, was installed in detuned form in several hundred 1928 JDH models, with 74 ci. These were considered the fastest production road vehicles of their time.

WALTER DAVIDSON
PRESIDENT

WILLIAM DAVIDSON
VICE PRESIDENT

WILLIAM HARLEY
CHIEF ENGINEER

ARTHUR DAVIDSON
SECRETARY

Six Outstanding Facts about Harley-Davidson

1. Harley-Davidson motorcycles, sidecars and parcelcars are sold and used in 116 countries.

2. Harley-Davidson motorcycles, sidecars and parcelcars are built in a factory that has 12 acres of floor space and employs 1800 people.

3. Harley-Davidson motorcycles and sidecars are used by over 2400 police and sheriff departments throughout the United States.

4. More dealers sell Harley-Davidsons than any other motorcycle in the world.

5. Harley-Davidson motorcycles are backed by twenty-three years of success.

6. Walter Davidson, President; William Davidson, Vice-President; William Harley, Chief Engineer; and Arthur Davidson, Secretary — the original founders of the Harley-Davidson Motor Company are still directing the affairs of the company.

HARLEY-DAVIDSON MOTOR COMPANY
MILWAUKEE, WISCONSIN

Printed in U. S. A.

In its first year of production, the single-cylinder Model A was still equipped with acetylene lamps and mechanical Klaxon horn. By 1927, both gadgets were no longer the "latest thing." Rated at 3.3 horsepower for tax purposes, the side-valve actually produced about 7 bhp.

Chapter 4

Side-valve flatheads

The 350 cc in side-valve or ohv form, first shown in 1926, marked a visible expansion of the Harley-Davidson model line-up. Although the factory had long shown, with its sports model and racing eight-valves, that it had mastered both design philosophies, the showrooms had contained only the ioe V-twin for the previous few years. The public associated the brand name only with the big V-twin motorcycle. Now, suddenly, there were four attractive singles in the stores.

During the development phase, Harley-Davidson designers had compared their design to several Indian Princes and European 350 cc machines, and they were satisfied with the results. The small side-valve had cast-iron pistons and was offered in two versions, the standard Model A with magneto ignition for $210, and the standard Model B with the Harley-Davidson single-unit electrical system for $235. In the decidedly quicker overhead-valve model, aluminum pistons were fitted. This was sold as the Sporting Model AA at $250 or Sporting Model BA at $275. For export, the Sporting Model AA was equipped with a clutch grip on altered handlebars and footrests instead of floorboards, making the Model AAE. The same applied to the electric Model BAE.

Two low-mounted camshafts drove the valvetrain of each model. The combustion chamber shape was again licensed from Ricardo, who was making millions for his pioneer work on cylinder head design. As Indian was dominating the interesting mid-range market with its Scout, which had caused Milwaukee's withdrawal of the Sports model (actually not a bad bike at all), Harley-Davidson wanted to regain lost ground in the realm of the single-cylinder machines. The new single garnered vital points against its market competitor, the Indian Prince.

From their experiences with the 350 cc side-valve single, the Milwaukee engineers derived the 750 cc V-twin with low-mounted camshafts. This 45 ci machine started its long run in 1929. As expected, the 1200 cc side-valve big twin followed a year later in 1930. The combustion chamber shape was licensed in writing by Ricardo, who also personally signed the receipts for royalties.

Side-valve engines are cheaper and easier to manufacture than ohv engines. To make mass production easier, the beloved ohv 350 cc motor was replaced by a 500 cc side-valve model in 1930. Yet although equipped like a 750, it was too weak.

During the depths of the Depression, prices for single-cylinder models were dropped. To

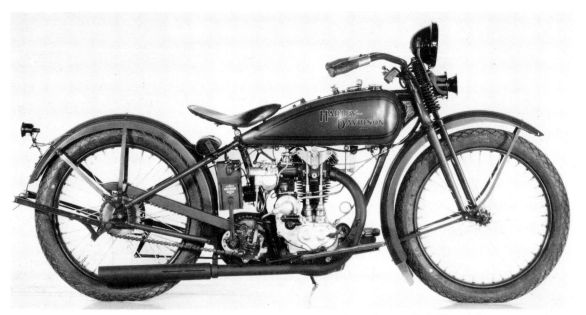

The faster, electric BA of 1927. Also in the three horse-power tax class, buyers could count on an actual 12 horses. The robust reliability of this motorcycle, and its single-unit electric system, was renowned.

Similarly equipped with Harley-Davidson electrics, the fast BAE of 1927 was a complete success in export markets. A 350 that ran over 60 mph and didn't break in the process was rare at that time.

stimulate sales, prices and profits on singles had to be cut to the lowest levels possible. The cost and effort expended in their manufacture made them real motorcycles, but sales results could not be compared to those of the expensive, prestigious twins. While the 1200 cc V big twin of 1932 commanded $320 plus freight, the standard 750 R at $295 was priced considerably lower. The 500 side-valve single brought in $235 plus freight; the similar 350 side-valve was knocked out at $195, for which price the front mudguard was replaced by a smaller one, and little more than the tool kit was left off. The 500 side-valve was also available with a Goulding sidecar, but few customers had the funds to buy one of these rigs, so it was soon dropped.

Similar fates awaited efforts to use the single for various utility vehicles. To offer new attractions for commercial and governmental clients, the busy Harley-Davidson engineers developed the Servi-Car with 45 ci power, and put it on the market in 1932. The following year,

1933, the company experienced an absolute low point with less than 4,000 units of all types sold. With their dealer margins, this represented less than $1 million of pre-tax gross sales; in other words, no profit, but rather a huge loss. That was probably the principal reason for the calculated move to tighten up the product line and cease production of the singles in 1934.

Ironically, fifty years later, many wish that Harley-Davidson would bring out a beautiful, powerful, reliable single for the 1980s and 1990s.

At the end of the 1920s, the fully developed Harley-Davidson J and F models seemed to be less fashionable than the four-cylinder machines from Henderson or the Indian Chiefs, despite regular improvements, strength and speed. Even the limited-production and quick 74 ci two-cam JDH machines couldn't change that. From a design standpoint, they were overshadowed by their competition, principally because the ioe Harley-Davidson big twin motor appeared little different from the Harley-David-

The 500 side-valve single was introduced in 1929. At the time, this 350 with a barely attainable 55 mph top speed was too lame even for younger buyers and those interested in mere transportation. In its introductory year, the price of $235 was still $40 above that of its older and still weaker sister. This photo demonstrates how simply the cylinder head could be removed and how easy care and maintenance were.

An early Harley-Davidson flathead prototype, known as the Silver Eagle, still very unfinished looking.

Model 30-V, the 74 ci big twin of 1930, which cost $340 at the factory. The price dropped in later years. It delivered 28 hp at the rear wheel, had a new, reinforced frame, a standard steering lock as a theft deterrent as even then Harleys were often stolen, two bullet lamps and, as accessories a speedometer, a larger clutch compared to the ioe engines and the unique exhaust. The factory touted this with "only one mile an hour slower than no exhaust, but so much quieter!"

Police version of the 74 ci big twin of 1930, with a rear-wheel-driven siren, first-aid kit, fire extinguisher and speedometer.

son V-twin of 1913. In terms of appearance and mechanicals, its character could hardly excite those American buyers who were looking for showier machines.

At that time, the car companies advertised the advantages of the then-dominant side-valve engines, the so-called flatheads. In the motorcycle industry, Indian promoted it as the best thing since sliced bread. After all, they had been concentrating on this design for some time. The ioe Harley engine, by comparison, seemed a relic of the past and was certainly no formula for success in surviving the economic hard times.

Starting in 1929, the relatively heavy 45 ci twins were marketed. These were unable to compete in the marketplace, however, with the lighter, quicker twins from Indian and Excelsior, the Scout and Super-X. In order to increase the demand for their products, the strategy in Milwaukee was to replace the honorable and long-lived J-series with the more modern big twin concept, the big side-valve, at about the time of introduction of the new single generation, or at the latest when the 750 twin came out. In the event, the new side-valve 74 ci engine, known as the Model V, as well as the higher-compression VL, was probably tested one year less than it should have been, and thrown into the marketplace one year too soon. The blame for this premature introduction can be placed on economic considerations.

Despite jubilant advertising claims touting the advantages and convenience of the new V models compared to the old J, the plant, the dealers and the customers experienced the teething troubles of the big twin from 1930 to 1932, and suffered many disappointments and warranty claims, news of which quickly spread by word of mouth. The machine could not be moved too quickly, for fear of damaging the valves, which received minimal oil spray lubrication.

With the Depression as the backdrop, Harley-Davidson found itself at the start of the thirties facing a difficult sell. The management was in an unenviable position. Sales figures slipped from over 20,000 in 1929 to the catastrophic results of 1933, with 3,700 machines sold. It is a

The forged VL fork provided about one inch more ground clearance, absorbed shocks better and also looked a bit different. Model J and JL owners often retrofitted it on their machines, and so brought the plant and the dealers a small profit in the dismal days of the early 1930s. For the big twins of 1936 and onward, it was too big for the steering head. It further lost popularity as later models came out with the longer springer fork, because you could hardly weld an extension into it.

wonder that the four founders continued; their actions cannot be explained by mere optimism or stubbornness. They all could have entered different careers, hocked their interests. It must have had something to do with an obsession for motorcycles. With that same obsession, they forced the refinement of their big twin, which, in the mid-thirties at the latest, could match the Indian Chief.

The new item for 1936 was the 80 ci flathead, a sort of Refrigerator Perry among motorcycles—large, good natured and enormously powerful, with more power in heart and soul than its slimmer, weaker twin, the 74 ci base model.

With the big Excelsior-Henderson, the Indian Ace Four as well as the Indian Big Chief and now with the new 45 and 74 ci Harley side-valves, something was becoming apparent, something that no one would have guessed a few years earlier at the presentation of the new singles. The design philosophies of the United States and Europe had hardly any remaining similarities. In the Old World, the Europeans were offering light, small-displacement, eco-

A sidecar rig of 1930, probably built for a country with left-hand traffic, consisting of a 1200 cc 30-V machine and 30-LT boat costing $110. Accessories included speedometer, steering damper, windscreen and lamp for the sidecar. In this trim, the potential customer would have to pay more than for a simple Ford Model T. Only in running and repair costs could the motorcycle offer advantages.

Model 32-R. The 45 ci engine, which had given rise to many complaints, was changed for 1932. Most apparent is the generator, which no longer appears as a third cylinder beside the front two; instead it is mounted between engine and frame, just like its larger brother. Among other things, aluminum pistons were fitted and the flywheels enlarged. $295 FOB Milwaukee.

nomical motorcycles as well as cars, at least in the lower-priced mass market.

The trend in Europe was to use innovative technical advances to get power by means of high revs from small-displacement engines, thereby reducing displacement-dependent taxes and insurance. In Europe, cars were far more expensive to obtain than a motorcycle or side-car, and operating costs played a totally different role. Distances in the small countries of Europe seemed laughable by comparison; cities were crisscrossed by roads and crowded each other.

Americans had no displacement tax, no mandatory insurance and hardly took notice of fuel costs; they were not restricted by crowding or bureaucracies. American designers followed the opposite goal—to get a minimal power output from the largest possible displacement at the lowest possible revs. The only thing of interest to them was high torque for effortless cruising over great distances. Their motor-driven vehicles appeared large, heavy and sturdy.

North America was endless, and for long distances, empty. In the United States, progress in road building had been made since the Great War. But when in 1933 the new president, Franklin D. Roosevelt, put previously unheard of sums of money into public works as part of his New Deal, the framework of today's road system began to rise. This provided not only jobs but also a calming influence and increased buying power. Against competition from inexpensive cars, the surviving motorcycle industry could keep only a small segment of the total vehicle market.

For Frank Schwinn, the chief of Excelsior, the motorcycle business was no longer profitable enough; he got out and concentrated on his profitable bicycle company. After the 1930s, only Harley-Davidson and Indian built motorcycles in the United States. Both were in trouble up to their necks. In Milwaukee, there was talk of laying the *Enthusiast* magazine to rest, but then it was decided to sell it for five cents per copy. The plant worked only a few days each week. The Wigwam, too, had financial and internal

troubles. The *Indian News* had not been in print for several years.

The AMA sanctioning body was also facing ruin. Indian, as well as virtually all parts suppliers, made it clear that they could do little to help. Without the financial and organizational assistance of the Harley-Davidson plant, the AMA would have shut down. It is not surprising that Milwaukee's influence in the organization grew.

At the beginning of the 1930s, financially responsible people at Harley-Davidson finally recognized a mistake made nearly fifteen years before: in the face of mass-produced and ever-cheaper cars, it was stupid, especially in regard to utility and value for the money, to manufacture motorcycles nearly as expensive as their four-wheeled competition. The car may have cost a few dollars more, but offered far more in the way of cargo space, comfort and prestige. A motorcycle would hardly be considered a family or company vehicle by any reasonable person. Motorcycles appealed less to the calculating buyer than to those looking for a fun vehicle.

With their marketing strategy emphasizing value, the boring olive paint work and sober advertising, Harley-Davidson was appealing to the wrong market segment, a fast-disappearing group of buyers. New attractive color combinations and tank designs were applied. The advertising campaign did an about-face.

Picnic at the beach, with two Flatheads and two couples. The photos in this series were taken on the Lake Michigan shore and appeared on the covers of the Enthusiast *for August 1932 and July 1933.*

As an outstanding motorcycle rider, William H. Davidson won many races. In 1930, riding his early Flathead, he became national enduro champion thanks to his decisive victory at the difficult Jack Pine cross-country race. This photo, taken at about that time, shows him on his personal specially equipped and well-maintained flathead. Note the reflections in the finish of the boat. Only 15 years later, he succeeded his uncle Walter Davidson as president of Harley-Davidson.

The 45 ci twin of 1933, then called the 33-R, could be picked up at the plant for $280. Depending on the location of the local dealer, delivery closer to home would cost a few dollars more in freight charges. For $10 more you could have the 33-RLD special sport solo model, with different head castings allowing the carburetor better access to the cylinders.

The frame of the 45 big twin of 1934, like all frames of that year, was made stronger, the clutch springs were larger and made of better material, breathing was only through Linkert carburetors, exhaust through the High-Flo Burgess muffler, a removable rear fender permitted easier wheel changes, the design was called Flying Diamond and the "airflow" taillight could also be ordered with a brake light.

The 45 ci twin of 1935 was delivered with the following changes: polished cylinder walls, slotted pistons, improved constant mesh transmission, more powerful rear brake, the "beehive" taillight first introduced in the Enthusiast and the downward-pointing exhaust deflector. The bike was painted in the so-called Flying Diamond design, available in five color combinations.

Weekend and sunshine. Who wouldn't want to trade
with our smiling friend?

Model year 1938. The Model 38-U, the medium-compression version of the 74 ci flathead. The Model US was essentially identical, except for gear ratios more suitable for sidecar operation; Model UL was the somewhat more expensive sports model. The 80 ci range, with virtually identical appearance, was labeled UH, UHS and, the cream of the crop, the high-compression ULH.

The 74 ci side-valve twin of 1940 with cast-iron heads. New features included the enlarged main bearings, the cooling or reinforcing ribs on the case cover, the half-round floorboards, the connected tank halves, which were easily regulated by means of the fuel valve on the upper left half, and the teardrop-shaped toolbox.

To promote a motorcycle exhibit, the Smithsonian Institution in Washington, D.C., altered an original Harley-Davidson poster announcing the new 45 ci Model D of 1929.

Harley-Davidson's olive-green routine ended in 1932 or 1933; Harleys were now supposed to promote an image of fun. Due to the difficult economic times, however, only a few thousand were sold.

BLACK AND
MANDARIN RED

THE 1933 HARLEY-DAVIDSON 74 BIG TWIN MODEL

The 74 ci Model U Flathead rig owned by Peter Wolf, better known as "Haunsi." Patient Haunsi has restored the bike perfectly several times after accidents. His stiff leg, the result of the most recent trip into the weeds, is now beginning to bend a bit easier, so he can again ride the 1200 cc machine solo. Eleven years ago, he and wife Lotte rode a Sportster to Nepal. All three returned safe, sound and wiser for the experience.

This is the first Harley Model E to leave the assembly line in 1936, personally inspected by the founders in a small ceremony. This special machine, with zero miles on the clock, is on display in the Harley-Davidson museum in York, Pennsylvania. The shape of the cylinder head covers of this 61 ci machine have given it the name Knucklehead.

Veteran bike meet in Tulare, California, 1986. Unfortunately, the immaculately restored 1947 1200 cc Knucklehead was far beyond my spending limit.

Clark Gable owned several Harleys, with which he took part in the California club scene of the thirties and forties. Behind his 1941 74 ci De Luxe Knucklehead is one of the trophies he won at amateur races and concours d'élégance.

Indian dealer Christian
Timmermann of Berlin,
Germany, comments on the
two exponents of the
American big twin
philosophy in the pre- and
postwar years: "The image
struggle between Harley and
Indian is almost like the plot
of a Western movie. The
Knucklehead impresses me,
but, instead of cheering for
the Midwestern cowboy, I'll
root for the Indian Chief."

Engine, transmission and
suspension of Uwe "Lucky"
Illgner's Knucklehead
chopper were more than 40
years old, with a few
overhauls behind them, when
the Harley restorer from
Friedberg, West Germany,
and wife Suzanne rode
straight across the United
States. Earlier, in the early
1970s, Illgner thrashed his
first Sportster all the way to
India.

Old warriors. For racing, originality sometimes suffers. "If tires like these had existed then, we would have mounted them. Why should we have less fun, riding around on old rubber, when these are available?" Indian Racing Scout and Harley-Davidson WR, competitors of the Class C era, on the Daytona infield, just prior to a match race.

The way this WLA is equipped (even the ammo box on the left side of the fork was full), its amiable owner is ready to depart Daytona Beach for the next war. He needn't even stop to shoot. The long bar on the Thompson submachine gun's butt was to be clamped under the rider's arm, to keep the barrel pointed more or less forward while the trigger was pulled.

*The first Panhead FL in the York,
Pennsylvania, museum.*

Uwe Illgner's Hydra-Glide.

These two old-timers, in Tulare,
California, 1986, must have checked
off every item in the accessory
catalogs, judging by the full dress of
their Harley-Davidson Duo-Glide and
Indian Big Chief. Timmermann,
Berlin's Indian expert, calls the big
Goulding sidecar the atom bomb,
which sort of fits into the spirit of its
time.

Wolfgang Hubner with his panhead
chopper: "I like 21 inch tires on the
chopper. With a six-inch fork
extension, my arms are horizontal, the
axle height is nearly identical to the
original, the weight distribution is
right, and it's stable in a straight line.
Curves are easy enough to take. The
good-looking SU carb sounds funny
because of its movable venturi noises,
but the engine runs better than with a
Linkert."

Hubner's brother, Peter, has just prepared this 1966 early Shovelhead for the German biannual inspection; now it's expected to obey when kicked to life.

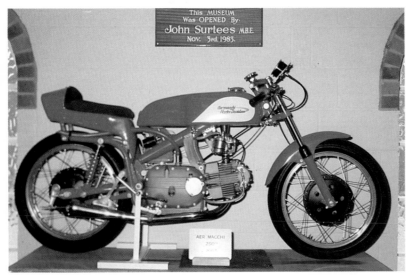

In the small motorcycle museum of multiple world trials champion Sammy Miller in southern England rests this early 1963 250 cc Aermacchi/Harley-Davidson Sprint racer with monotube frame. Its pushrod engine was competitive well into the era of Japanese bikes. Its weak spots were workmanship, electrics and so on.

The Great American Freedom Machine. During the AMF epoch, just about everything imaginable was produced and marketed. This thing appeared in 1972 and was called the Shortster, with a displacement of 65 cc, magneto ignition and three speeds. The sales literature called it one of the "Harley-Davidson Out-Performers." The 1975 record sales of 70,000 Harleys takes on a quite different meaning when this machine is considered.

The 45 ci WL of 1947. Although British bikes were beginning to make themselves known, things were picking up from the production lows of the immediate pre- and postwar period. New features included the altered shift pattern, the new instrument panel and the tombstone taillight. The front hydraulic shock assisted the springer fork. Three color combinations were offered, the need for chrome recognized and prices slightly raised.

A 1947 750 cc flathead with aluminum cylinder heads and teardrop (or egg-shaped) toolbox.

This is the Model 38 WL, the 45 ci machine with the lighter Goulding sidecar and frame, built in 1938. The sidecar is sprung by a rear transverse leaf spring, a small leaf spring on the sidecar's wheel and two front coil springs. Apparently an Anglophile export model, for left-hand traffic.

Military service

William Harley, a US Army inspector and Walter Davidson in August 1931, at the office entrance of the Motor Company, with two WLs bound for Army service. The founders offered this robust and easily maneuvered WL model to the Army, convinced it was the right basis for a military motorcycle. The military, on the other hand, decided on the later Model WLA, essentially the same as the WL, after several expensive and unnecessary detours.

A motorcycle, jeep and truck column of the 107th Cavalry Regiment, moving out.

This half-pint panzer is entered in the company archives under "Automatic Colt Machine Gun." It was probably ordered in 1940 by the armory at Ft. Knox, Kentucky, as an experimental machine. Underneath all that armor is an 80 ci flathead. Because the skirting really did consist of armor plate, the torquey 1340 cc engine was more than sensible. Still, it probably wasn't a real road rocket.

An open-air tank which never had a chance to make the enemy run—or laugh. The US Marines used a few of these Harley tanks in the thirties while based in Shanghai, China.

The 1941 WLA for the US Army. With its bright aluminum heads, which transferred heat better than the cast-iron heads, the 45 ci motor developed 25 hp from a 6:1 compression ratio. The iron heads were only available with 4.75:1 compression.

Four, three, two, one, ignition. The trainee rider, concentrating mightily, is assisted on his first trip by two driving instructors. His buddies, waiting their turns in back, seem to be enjoying his discomfort. US Army driving school, 1941.

The 1942 WLC was the WLA for Canadian Army service. Instead of the baggage carrier, the WLC's rear fender was crowned by a saddle with ample spring travel.

100

Another Canadian contract was for this Knucklehead combination, intended to drive a scout car. Air cooling of the cylinders, located behind the differential in an enclosed engine compartment, may explain the reason why this arrangement never saw service.

Manufacture of this trike would probably have been more preferable to the Milwaukee firm. Twenty-five to 40 of this design, with Knucklehead, shaft- or chain-drive, right-mounted shifter, and disc wheels, were built for evaluation by the US Army in 1940. The fork is somewhat longer, and was later used on the XA. Instead of this pleasing three-wheeler, the Army opted for the Jeep, which has since proven its worth.

The director of the service school, J. P. Ryan (at right), photographed at the plant in April 1943 with civilian employees of the US Army, learning the intricacies of the WLA.

Something special—Model XA/XS of 1943 with driven sidecar, the driveshaft to the third wheel serving also as a stressed member of the hack's frame. Milwaukee's engineers had no problems with driveshaft design, but weren't particularly impressed with the concept. After the war Harley-Davidson decided to use driveshafts strictly for utility vehicles, for ease of maintenance.

US Army driver training, 1943. Military driving schools put special emphasis on transitions between varied terrain. This student was in the process of learning that WLAs were easier to manage on asphalt than on sand.

A display window at Niss, a Milwaukee furniture store, 1942, featuring the famous Harley-Davidson Blitz-bike, a displayed WLA, a saluting image of Gen. Douglas MacArthur, the call to buy war bonds and reminder of the five employees in service.

Civilian chores

In the period from the 1920s to the 1940s, it was customary for auto dealerships to pick up and deliver cars for repair and maintenance. The Hollywood, California, Packard dealership tested this elaborate single-cylinder arrangement (below) for its pickup service; with this the plant was experimenting with an alternative to the three-wheeler. However, with the auxiliary wheels out, it was simply too unstable, and therefore did not go into production. Instead, the factory decided to concentrate on the 750 cc WL-based Servi-Car, which went into production in 1932.

The unusual frame at the front of the Servi-Car was for attachment to the rear bumper of the tow car.

If you want to sell motorcycles in hard times, you'll need to think of new uses. This was a fitting utility vehicle for Roosevelt's road-building programs. The guide bar at the left assisted the driver in keeping the right distance from the curb. The paint cycle was changeable, allowing painting of passing and no-passing zones. When it got too dark to see, the crew could head for a bar and down a bottle of Old Heidelberg.

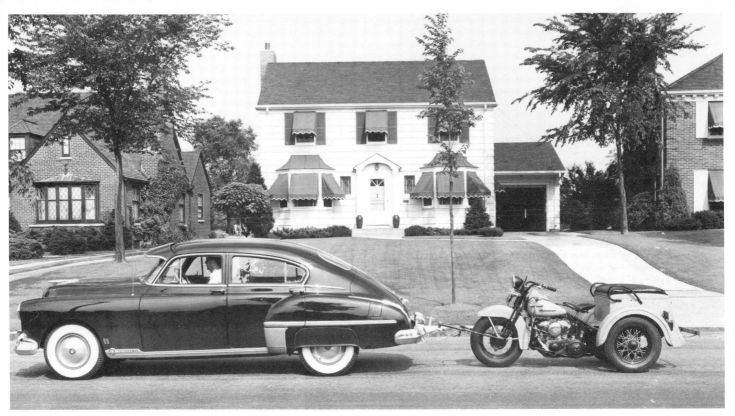

The auto mechanic would ride the Servi-Car to the
client's house, pick up the car and tow the Servi-Car
back to his shop.

Servi-Car in service. The officer need not even stoop to
perform his chores.

With the cargo box removed, the enclosed drive chain and differential, sprung rigid axle, combination of leaf and coil springing, dual rear brakes and large muffler are visible. The relatively complex structure of the Servi-Car is impressive.

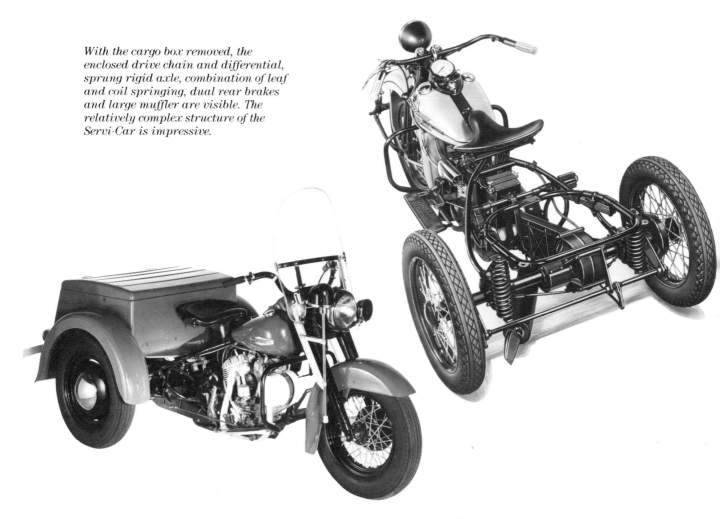

Servi-Car for police duty with lights, siren and windscreen. Mid-1960s.

Servi-Car as a truck tractor. This project never went past the prototype stage, since the 750 cc engine, with only 25 hp, was too weak to move heavily laden trailers.

108

Chapter 5

Peashooter and WR

Beginning in 1926, privateer riders, mounted on Harley-Davidson 350 cc single-cylinder ohv racers, the Peashooters, began winning national titles. Peashooters often proved victorious even against stiff competition from the 750 cc ohv and side-valve machines, the heavy 1340 cc side-valves and the ioe hillclimbers. The tiny 350 cc Peashooters, the similar Indian Princes, and, soon, the 750 cc side-valve racing twins from both companies—the WR and the Sport Scout—offered amateurs fully developed production racers at attractive prices.

A new concept in racing rules had been under discussion since the late twenties. The interest on the part of manufacturers to enter cost-no-object competition had long since faded, as the costs were far too high for the minimal returns. There was an unspoken agreement regarding this restraint on behalf of the manufacturers. The sport was to become financially bearable for the companies as well as more attractive for unsponsored riders.

The AMA, in preparing its rules for the so-called Class C, recognized that many parties interested in the sport possessed fast, lightweight European 500 cc ohv machines, which were probably superior to the larger side-valves. As of 1934, with the introduction of the Class C racing formula, the rules stipulated that the side-valve engines, handicapped by rev limits, compression and combustion chamber shape when compared to the higher-performance ohv machines, were to be granted a displacement advantage: 500 cc ohv engines were to compete directly with 750 cc side-valves.

All of this is a brief introduction to the popular racing scene of the late 1930s and the immediate postwar years, in which the two surviving manufacturers, Harley and Indian, were not directly involved, but rather represented by countless talented tuners and nonprofessional riders.

In the mid-twenties, organizers, amateur riders and manufacturers were interested in letting the battles of attrition waged in the Class A era die quietly, at least on short courses. Following the examples set by Indian and Excelsior, Harley-Davidson began making its 350 cc production racers in 1926. The little machines were not all that slow on the short tracks; speeds in excess of 90 mph were measured.

In the thirties, Joe Petrali was the only true Harley-Davidson works pilot. He won numerous races and championships riding the Peashooters which he helped develop. Petrali's name stood for Harley-Davidson victories, Harley-Davidson records and Harley-Davidson racing machines.

Joe Petrali, just prior to a dirt-track race, astride his 21 ci racer. Two low-mounted camshafts actuate the overhead valves via pushrods to power this rev-happy plant, equipped with dual exhausts and magneto ignition, all mounted in a well-handling, light machine.

The small, light, high-revving Harley-Davidson singles soon established their dominance on the short American dirt tracks. As an intelligent, easy choice for many hillclimbs, they even triumphed against the Class A climbers which were twice as powerful. In this photo, a 1928 track racer with extended intake pipe and split exhaust port.

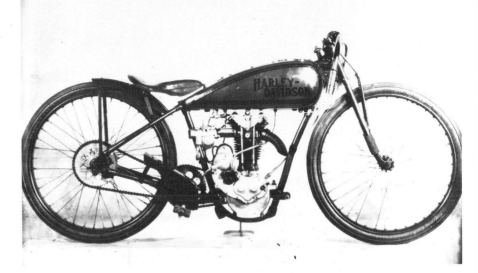

A 350 cc Peashooter of 1928 with modified frame, three-speed transmission, Schebler Indianapolis barrel carburetor, split exhaust port, dual brakes and footboards. Probably an export model for road racing. In England, Australia, New Zealand, Sweden and other countries, the 350 cc bikes soon became popular thanks to their successes against larger-displacement competitors on grass-track, speedway and road-racing circuits in the below 500 cc class. The Peashooters were considered hard to beat. But the competition never rests; particularly in England, Rudge and JAP were close behind.

Now here's an interesting piece. The year of manufacture, 1930, has been established as the type designation 30 CAF. Connie Schlemmer, writing in Antique Motorcycle, the publication of the Antique Motorcycle Club of America, thinks it may have evolved from the CAC flat-track racer. In any case, it was built in a very limited series, and is generally considered a 500 cc street racer for the European market. Schlemmer does not exclude the possibility of several models having been sent to Japan. He has restored a similar model, with a stretched frame and only 350 cc, which had been run by works rider Herb Reiber in the 1930 hillclimb season, in which its light weight drew considerable attention.

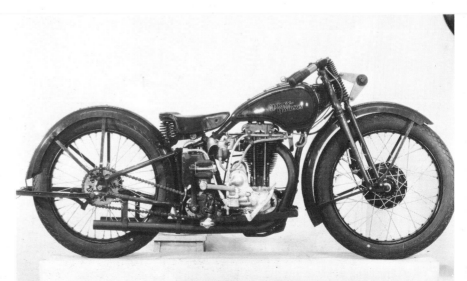

Regardless, here we see Herb Reiber reaching the summit of the August 1940 Muskegon Hill Climb, mounted on his 45 ci ohv hillclimber.

Bill Connelly and Fred Danrieam, with their 80 ci flathead rig, established a transcontinental record of 69 hours, 42 minutes and 17 seconds, an hour and 34 minutes faster than the old solo record. Their record still stands today.

Leo Anthony with his 1938 WRTT street racer, still equipped with the forged VL fork. Many Class C racers owned only one machine, which they piloted in road races as well as on tracks. For flat-track races, such as here at the Milwaukee Mile, Anthony simply disconnected the brakes.

The Milwaukee State Fair Race, August 23, 1947. The Milwaukee course was a classic one-mile track. The leader, Number 7, Floyd Emde, is really stretching his steel-shod leg out.

It apparently paid off. Floyd Emde of San Diego, California, and his wife are happy that he's won the Ten Miles National Championship. The rear cylinder of his WR is especially interesting.

"Babe" Tancrede, a motorcycle officer, bore the number-one plate of a short-course champion in 1941. Here he has just won the 1941 flat-track weekend at Laconia. Shaking hands, at left, is reported to be John Harley, later parts and production manager in Milwaukee.

Lowell Rettinger, yet another of the many national champions who was successful against the Indian Race Scouts and British ohv twins. Harley-Davidson has won the most US Grand National Championships to the present day.

Paul Albrecht of Sacramento, California, aboard his WR, was 1948 five-mile dirt-track champion of the half-mile courses.

The popular Leo Anthony, here on the Milwaukee track, won several national championships. He altered the works equipment of his 1947 racer, using hand clutch and foot shifter instead.

The WR of 1950. The racing magneto between the cylinders was valued for its stronger spark. The steering head has been given lightening holes, and a stiffening member has been welded into the rear of the frame.

Production chief William Davidson (back row, left), chief designer William Harley (back row, right) and Service School director J. P. Ryan (front row, right). This photo may be a Service School class graduation picture, or more likely a portrait of the foremen of various departments. From the 1930s.

Harleys didn't entirely sell themselves; dealers and agents had to help. Graduation picture of a class at the Sales School, from the 1930s. Fourth from left in back row: Walter Davidson.

Chapter 6

An epoch begins: the V-twin

As one leafs through old motorcycle magazines, books and reports in an attempt to get a feel for the thirties, astounding thoughts come forth. After 1932, Harley-Davidson's technical teething troubles with the 1200 cc flathead had been overcome. Compared to the Indian Chief, the machine was saleable as well as competitive, and soon outsold the Chief.

Even in the thirties, the purchase of a motorcycle was an emotional decision: "Do I like this thing, or not?" Rational aspects did not play the main role in the decision. Most buyers decided on a Harley or an Indian flathead according to how they reacted to their differing concepts, and according to what circles the purchaser moved in. If for no other reason, your friends or marque club determined whether the decision would be in favor of the Hog or Honest Injun.

Those who changed brands would probably also have to change their social circles. Harley-Davidson benefited from a loyal and patient clientele, whose faith was alternately rewarded or tested by various moves on the part of dealers or factory. The manufacturers could count on a firm base of repeat customers; on the other hand, with the diminished buying power of the times, radical new products could hardly win new customers.

With the outstanding little Peashooters, which had dominated their classes on the world's race courses, the designers in Milwaukee had proven their mastery of the conversion from side-valve to overhead-valve motors. In their arsenal were two side-valve motors, in the 45 as well as the 74 ci classes, which, despite a few weak points, were nothing to be ashamed of.

If the designers were to take these proven powerplants and replace the side valves with pushrods and new cylinder heads containing rocker arms and overhead valves, they could take advantage of a sure-fire recipe for a successful new motorcycle type. An ohv engine would have a distinctly higher power output and more rugged characteristics, compared to its side-valve progenitor.

With a design department worthy of the title, and enriched by the talents of respected names like Bill Harley, Bill Ottaway, Joe Petrali and Hank Syvertsen, we may assume that this project was thoroughly tested in the prototype phase. After the introduction of the flatheads, rumors began to circulate that an ohv Harley was due soon. Indeed, in short order a fast motor of that type did appear, a 750 cc ohv driven by four low-mounted cams, with dual exhausts. It was sold in limited numbers in 1930 to racers for hillclimbing and foreign road races.

It was even sold in a new frame, which proved itself in the hard tests of racing.

Why the engineers did not develop the new motor for a civilian street model remains unknown. The designers would have saved a great deal of time and development work with such an ohv motor for their normal sales range, as well as the possibility of teething troubles expected from a brand-new design. Most components of the flathead-derived ohv were proven parts. They remained unchanged, and therefore the production process and manufacturing steps did not need to undergo an expensive and complicated restructuring, as the various versions of this motor differed in only a few details. The immense costs of a completely new development could thus be reduced. In view of the general market lethargy and the associated brutal competition of the car companies, this was not merely a good idea, but rather a compelling argument.

The leaders of the Harley-Davidson Motor Company also could have brought out brilliant new designs. Unfortunately, we have photos only of the 750 cc racers, and none of prototypes for the potential street version (at least, none that I can find). Instead, those responsible, over fifty years ago, chose the more expensive path, and developed a new long-stroke ohv motor. It's tempting to think that the three Davidsons and Bill Harley told themselves that if they were to remain in this uncomfortable business, then at least they would have fun at it.

The necessary step of further fragmenting production was taken in stride. In the new ohv engine, the cylinders were angled at forty-five degrees to one another, a low-mounted camshaft actuated rocker arms in the cylinder head by means of four pushrods of differing lengths, which in turn actuated the valves. Everything was enclosed, which at that time was not always a given. The head, like diverse other parts, was a fine example of the foundryman's art. In the drive section, the engineers for the first time used pressure lubrication instead of the total-loss system used previously. Roller bearings were also used extensively. Other new items included the double-loop tubular frame, four-speed transmission, tank-mounted instrument panel and chrome-moly front fork.

By means of investment incentives, price and production controls, as well as new laws, President Roosevelt guided the economy. In 1934, overtime work was made more difficult to obtain; instead, employers were expected to hire more workers. Back in Milwaukee, in principle, the Knucklehead was ready in 1934. Testing of prototypes and preparation for production were to be more thorough for this model, and carried through by the well-practiced team.

Somewhere along the line, government representatives or vindictive labor unions not represented at Harley-Davidson were watching, and turned the infraction of the overtime guideline into a scandal. Hundreds of new employees would have to be hired, and the work was hardly progressing. The long-awaited baby did not

118

come into the world in 1935, as had been planned. Rumors spread of a new ohv V-twin Harley-Davidson and its imminent appearance or demise, beginning in 1934 or 1935.

In a surprise move, the factory brought out its new E-series in 1936. The impressed customers accepted early lubrication problems. The motors, with their overhead valves, would accept heavier loads and withstood high temperatures better, thanks to a centrifugal oil pump and an engine-speed-dependent oil pressure relief valve. This was closed at high rpm to ensure maximum lubrication, and opened at low rpm. In this way, the oil was circulated around the transmission and was led back to the oil tank.

The new machine, soon known as the Knucklehead, was aesthetically pleasing and proved to be a delight to ride, which won new friends for American motorcycles. Over the next twelve years—indeed to the present day—its appearance and technology have been changed only in minor details, and then only with discretion. Its visual components, including rigid, unsprung frame (hard tail), the frame loops which fit closely around the motor (which needed its own unique fuel tank, due to its increased height), the horseshoe oil tank, fishtail exhaust, fork and fenders as well as the tasteful paint work all fit together and formed the image of the classic motorcycle for future generations.

Harley-Davidson had found its style and its classic ohv V-twin motor. In 1941, the plant presented its 1200 cc version with high hopes. Yet Harley was having problems with the Japanese even then, as they marred the first year of the big Knucklehead with their attack on Pearl Harbor and the ensuing war. In 1942, only a few 1200 cc Knuckleheads were built. The 1941 and 1942 models are highly regarded due to their outstanding quality.

The nickname "Knucklehead" comes from the shape of the covering for the valve mechanism on the cylinder head, the rocker box, which resembles the shape of the knuckle of the hand. Of course, its builders gave the ohv its own proper names, according to engine or transmission particulars. The family name E was used to designate all 61 ci motors. The E, without following letters, was the plain vanilla model: 1000 cc, low compression. EL indicated the higher-compression Special Sport Solo; ES was the sidehack model, with reverse gear if desired. The larger-displacement 74 ci clan got the next letter in the alphabet, F. Types F, FL and FS were named like their smaller cousins.

Production director William A. Davidson passed away in 1937. His brother, company president Walter Davidson, died in 1942, followed by Bill Harley in 1943. As the culmination of their life's work, the founders each had carved their own monument in their own lifetimes.

In the next years, the plant produced mainly WLAs. During the war, civilians could buy vehicles only by special permit. The development department continued to work on the Knucklehead, which liked to leak oil. All efforts proved to be a little less than satisfactory, so the motor was redesigned. The Knucklehead was followed in 1948 by the Panhead, of basically similar design but with improved valvetrain and lubrication. The Panhead, too, retained its classic appearance, until its replacement in 1965 by the early Shovelhead, which again featured a modernized cylinder head.

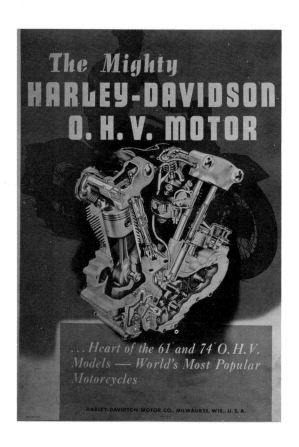

The first year of the 61 ci ohv motor was 1936. Vital statistics were bore 84 mm, stroke 87 mm. The engine developed 40 horses at 4800 rpm, ten more than the 74 ci flathead. The curb weight was 564 lb.

The 61 ci ohv twin of 1937, Model 37 EL (in Single Sport form) or Model 37 E with lower compression. The photo was later retouched by a graphic artist for advertising purposes, and showed the pilot flashing through a sunny countryside, with the wheels blurred by motion.

A classic frame, light handling, low saddle position and enormous torsional rigidity are a few of the positive virtues of the reinforced Straightleg frame of the 1937 big twins.

121

After the cast parts of Knucklehead or flathead frames were welded into place, the frames were annealed to eliminate stress. The frames of other models, the forks, seat tubes, crash bars and con- necting members for Servi-Cars were also brazed. The frame department was loud and hot, the frames glowed orange and the welding torches roared. Photo taken in 1939.

In this department, the sheet metal bodies of sidecars and Servi-Cars were assembled. In view of the total sales of 8,000 solo bikes of all types in 1939, this view of the less desirable sidehacks must represent a significant part of the annual production.

And this is how the Knucklehead appeared with sidecar.

A storeroom as well stocked with 61 ci Knuckleheads as this one would be the envy of many an enthusiast. I, for one, would even make my living room wall available for this. Taken in 1939, in the engine storeroom, where engines awaited installation in frames.

The drive gears exposed, without their well-formed cover.

Model 38 EL, a 61 ci Special Sport Solo of 1938. The covering of the rocker arms was altered to make the head quieter and cleaner, and synthetic rubber seals made it oil tight. It should be noted that the works continued to further improve the cylinder head area of the Knucklehead.

On a small side street of San Francisco, a task force of the San Francisco Police Department, using motorcycles and car, is patrolling, alert yet at ease, to serve and protect the citizens. Perhaps the better equipment of the lead bike indicates that it is being ridden by the group's leader.

And in 1939, things got more elegant, American style. From this year onward, the Knucklehead was available in two (Sport or De Luxe) and later three (Utility, Sport or De Luxe) equipment levels. The expensive De Luxe accessory package dressed the Knucklehead in handsome traveling clothes, with noteworthy bags, crash bars, auxiliary headlamps, brake and front fender lights, concho saddle and other bric-a-brac.

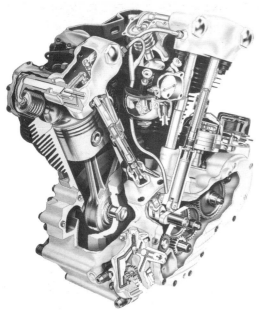

Phantom drawing of the Knucklehead motor. Of interest is the fire ring at the top of the cylinder wall, which was not found on all Knuckleheads and was designed to eliminate blown head gaskets.

The California Highway Patrol, a steady Harley customer, put 40 radio-equipped 61 ci police models into service in 1938.

With the 1940 model, the engineers changed rocker shafts and rocker arms for better lubrication, enlarged the cooling fins on the cylinders and, while they were at it, finned the crankcase covers.

126

*Are we having fun on our 61?
Or is this a 1200? In sunshine
and countryside, 1941, the
last summer of peace.*

*Dressed in an outfit selected
from the Harley-Davidson
catalog, our friend sits
astride an equally well-
dressed 1941 61 ci E or EL,
equipped with optional
saddlebags and rear crash
bar. Those who ordered just
the Utility model could spend
a few extra bucks to put
together an upgraded
accessory package from the
catalog.*

One of the last Knucklehead motors. The redesigned oil pump has an additional drive wheel which prevents too much oil from being slung into the crankcase at low revs.

Meanwhile, the task force has gotten a call via the Harley-Davidson-developed motorcycle radios, and rushes to the scene with lights, sirens and wide-open throttles, to prevent the worst or at least nab the culprits.

That's it, then. The Knucklehead performed its last act in 1947. In its 74 ci form it had been renamed FL and was more popular than the original EL. The shift gate and shift pattern were changed in that year, front and rear crash bars were standard, as were a new, flatter instrument panel as well as the tombstone taillight to meet the lighting requirements of most states. The addition of a front hydraulic shock absorber softened the aging springer fork, but the long-awaited hydra fork would have to wait until the coming of the Panhead in 1949. The accessory trade meanwhile had a thriving business supplying telescopic forks for Harleys.

Chapter 7

The style develops: the Panhead

Due to the war and raw material rationing, the planned replacement of the Knucklehead was delayed. Finally, in 1948, the reworked version, the ohv Panhead of 61 and 74 ci, appeared on the market. The springer fork was used for one last year. Total Harley-Davidson sales of 30,000 bikes in its introductory year were acceptable, and the Panhead had its part in that number. Yet until production ceased in 1965, the model seldom saw annual sales figures of more than 6,000 Panhead-equipped big twins, compared to total annual Harley-Davidson sales of, at best, 15,000.

The postwar sales slump had varying explanations. One was that the attractive prices of British competitors brought large numbers of British bikes into the country. After the war, the freight rates of the large number of freighters began to climb. Also, the import tariffs were especially low in the United States, seldom exceeding five percent. Importers of British bikes were seasoned pros, like Floyd Clymer and Alf Child, who had worked for or with Harley-Davidson. They were well aware of mistakes and weak points on the part of Harley-Davidson and used their knowledge to the utmost. Also, they offered small- and medium-size motorcycles, against which Harley-Davidson had no competitive product.

The superior reliability and technology, the many racing successes and the prestigious image provided Harleys with an outstanding reputation overseas, and knowledgeable bikers preferred them. Between the wars, the plant was able to sell a significant part of its production there. The designers of the British, German and Italian competition were not asleep at the switch, and by the 1930s were offering increasingly outstanding, technically innovative products. After the war, Harleys were certainly no worse in quality or reputation, but the export situation had worsened dramatically.

Europe and Asia were largely destroyed in the war. For the time being, those countries would have other matters on their minds. Those who still thought of fine motorcycles were forced to buy the local products due to high import duties. Last but not least, the Marshall Plan had helped to rebuild the partially bombed-out British bike industry and had modernized at least the manufacturing process. In Germany, the demolished plants and large service networks of BMW and NSU rose from the ashes, which, with their modern, affordable machines, often made life difficult for small-time importers.

Countries that had at one time provided export markets, such as Poland and Czechoslovakia, were suddenly cut off from the world

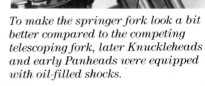

To make the springer fork look a bit better compared to the competing telescoping fork, later Knuckleheads and early Panheads were equipped with oil-filled shocks.

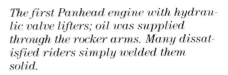

The first Panhead engine with hydraulic valve lifters; oil was supplied through the rocker arms. Many dissatisfied riders simply welded them solid.

On the table in Pohlmann's photo studio. In spite of questionable stability, these two seem happy; I'm beginning to see why photographic models are so well paid. The first ohv Panheads of 1948 were, like their predecessors, available in 61 and 74 ci versions. The springer fork was in its last year.

The 1948 odometer is still on zero miles. In the next 17 years, to 1965, it was followed by many more.

The 1948
HARLEY-DAVIDSONS
Biggest Motorcycle Story of the Year

Hydraulic Valve Lifters on O.H.V. Engines
Chrome Plated Covers on O.H.V. Rocker Arms
Aluminum Heads on O.H.V. Models
Additional O.H.V. Engine Improvements
Edge-lighted Speedometer Dial on All Models
Bonderizing Features 1948 Models
Theft-proof Lock on Big Twins
Terminal Box on All Models
Improved Big Twin Frame
New-type Clutch Pedal on Servi-Cars
New Offset Tow Bar on Servi-Cars
More Chrome Items Available,
Comfortable, Latex-filled Solo Saddle Available
Eight Equipment Groups
Three Color Options:
    Azure Blue, Flight Red, Brilliant Black

★

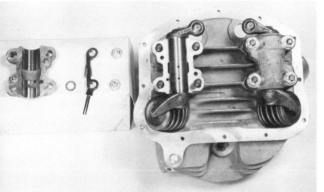

The rear cylinder head of the Panhead. The inlet rocker arm is disassembled; the tiny guide tube supplies oil mist to the inlet valve.

Harley-Davidson provided its big twins with a telescoping fork in 1949; the top-of-the-line model has since been known as the Hydra-Glide. Detroit, too, gave its products similarly pretty names, Dyna-Glide for example. Milwaukee stuck with the tradition of giving its motorcycles a typical, descriptive first name, usually followed by the Glide family name.

market. Many erstwhile export markets such as the Dutch East Indies, Indonesia, India, Burma and Malaysia, as former colonies, wanted to develop their native industries and therefore kept imports away. For that reason they erected tax barriers that could only be scaled by financial high jumpers.

Even police departments in the United States and abroad, normally a reliable market for both factory and dealers, increasingly bought cars instead of motorcycles. Tens of thousands of military surplus WLA machines were thrown onto the already saturated market at ridiculously low prices. Normally good sales territories such as the Netherlands were thus blocked for nearly a decade.

Company president William H. Davidson, known for his quiet optimism, yet managed to motivate his followers. For the dealer conventions, which lasted several days, a large hotel in Milwaukee was usually rented, in which the dealers could find lodging at reasonable rates. In the large, decorated conference room, William H. Davidson would deliver his report on the current fiscal year, followed by criticisms, insights and outlooks of the vice-presidents, after which the meeting would be opened to discussion.

At some point in the proceedings, to musical accompaniment, the curtains would part, revealing the spotlighted models of the next model year. After exclamations, aahs and oohs, discussion or applause, the attendees could wander to alcoves or nearby rooms to view accessories and related programs. Early orders were rewarded with convenient terms. To bring the conventiongoers together and to strengthen the Harley-Davidson esprit de corps, excursions, cultural events, plant tours, dinners and dances were organized.

It wasn't too difficult to keep the Harley dealers in line. They well knew that Harley-Davidson jealously allowed no other goods before them in the showrooms; besides, they generally had bigger profit margins than their Anglo-Saxon or Indian colleagues. But Harley-Davidson didn't give things away either, and the

Harley-Davidson was and remains an important economic and social factor in Milwaukee. It must not have been difficult to convince the city fathers to decorate the tower of City Hall for the 1951 dealer convention. In the mid-fifties, the welcome shone out at night; lightbulbs had been installed in the white letters.

132

stacks of dollar bills did not exactly fall into their pockets.

In the immediate postwar and Panhead year, Milwaukee management expected them to sell the 61 and 74 ci big twin, in Knucklehead form to 1948, thereafter as the Panhead, with the 61 ci or 1000 cc version being laid to rest in 1954, without replacement, after seventeen years of production. There was no fundamental difference in insurance or taxation between the two sizes; besides, the 74 was more popular. So why not simplify the manufacturing process, which had been split into two engine sizes, but which cost the same for both models? Also, there was less profit in the 1000 cc bikes.

In its second year of 1949, the Panhead finally got its hydraulic front fork and was known as the Hydra-Glide. From 1953 onward, the hydraulic tappets, previously working directly on the rocker arms, were repositioned below the pushrods. In 1958, having been given rear shock absorbers, the bike lost the Hydra-Glide name, its riders lost their fear of railroad crossings and the machines were then called Duo-Glide. In 1965, the last year of the Panhead, life became simpler for those who could not or would not fall or slide onto the Harley kick-starter, thanks to the introduction of the twelve-volt electrical system and electric starter.

The big twin was the flagship of the company and, thanks to a healthy dealer profit margin, usually brought respectable sums into the dealers' accounts. Customers gladly equipped their touring Panheads with items from the large (and profitable) accessory catalog. Every dealer endeavored to sponsor not only a local Harley club, but also a full dresser club, to watch them grow and prosper.

The GE 750 Servi-Car with its small side-valve motor was a utility vehicle, a quiet but steady seller, equipped with the same engine that had been installed in the 45 ci WL model up to 1952. The WL was replaced by the new Model K, also with 750 cc, which in turn was replaced by the 1954 Model KH with 55 ci. These middle-class singles sometimes sold quite handsomely, but relief from financial woes did not arrive until 1957, with the 883 cc Sportster.

To cater to the market for small motorcycles, which had been going exclusively to the European makers, Harley-Davidson copied the small German DKW RT and began selling the attractive 125 cc two-stroke in 1947. Given a telescopic fork, in 1951 it was named Tele-Glide; a year later, displacement was increased to 165 cc for more power. The two-strokes were well liked in their unique market segment, but their pricing and dealer markup were of necessity low.

May, 1957   21

HARLEY-DAVIDSON OFFICERS ADVANCED

W. J. HARLEY

W. C. DAVIDSON

DIRECTORS of the Harley-Davidson Motor Company advanced three officers in a recent meeting. William H. Davidson, president, announced the following changes in the company's top management:

William J. Harley was advanced to vice president, engineering; Walter C. Davidson advances to vice president, sales; and Otto P. Resech becomes the secretary and treasurer of the company.

Harley is a son of William S. Harley, one of the original founders of the company. A graduate in mechanical engineering at the University of Wisconsin, Harley joined the firm in 1934, became a director in 1937 and treasurer in 1943. He is a member of the Society of Automotive Engineers.

Davidson is also a son of an original founder, Walter Davidson. He joined the firm in 1936, became a director in 1943 and secretary in 1951.

Joining the firm as an accountant in 1934, Resech became assistant secretary in 1950 and a director in 1952. He is a member of the National Office Managers Association.

Gordon M. Davidson continues as vice president, manufacturing; and J. J. Balsom continues as the company's controller.

Spexarth Promoted to Chief Engineer

William J. Harley, vice president, engineering, has announced the promotion of Chris Spexarth to the position of chief engineer. Chris is an honor graduate of Marquette University, receiving his degree in mechanical engineering in 1931. He came directly to Harley-Davidson, became a designer in 1933, chief designer in 1937 and assistant engineer in 1943. He is also a member of the Society of Automotive Engineers.

C. SPEXARTH

O. P. RESECH

In the old Juneau Avenue plant, carts were pushed from one work station to another and there were frequent back-ups. Because different models were produced simultaneously, the line workers had to keep a large number of parts on hand.

For that reason, a massive parts inventory was required. But even the outstanding spare parts organization filled the warehouse to the rafters and required the services of many knowledgeable people.

For each of the 50 years, a motorcycle. Each year, the collection was enlarged by adding one of the current models. Until the late sixties, this museum was the high point of a plant tour.

A ride in the country, I would guess 1950 or 1951.

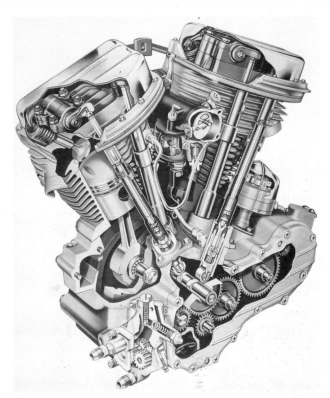

Happy faces, thanks to the customers; those assembled around a mockup of the Panhead motor are apparently satisfied with its appearance and technology. At the Harley-Davidson dealer convention, Milwaukee, 1952. Dot and Earl Robinson, Detroit dealers, are standing at left.

From 1953, the hydraulic lifters were repositioned below the pushrods. One of the fine details that Harley-Davidson generously gave to the motor heads of the world (well, they could buy it) and which is still being rediscovered by other firms. From 1953, there remained only the 74 ci ohv big twin. The 61 ci model was discontinued after a production run of 17 years as Knucklehead and Panhead.

Anniversary medallion of 1954.

Tank emblem of 1957-1958.

Six years after the introduction of rear suspension with the Model K, the big twin for 1958 also was given a rear swing arm with dual springs and shocks and was thereafter dubbed Duo-Glide. This model includes risers and stainless-steel fork tube covers.

The Duo-Glide's straight-leg frame with curved swing arm, frame break under the seat and retention of the saddle supported by a spring in the frame tube.

Whatever became of this couple and their 1960 Duo-Glide? The newly styled headlamp looks on, unperturbed.

Base model of the 1962 Duo-Glide range.

23596

The base model apparently wasn't enough for the owner of this Duo-Glide; he bought more accessories. Still, he must have been running out of money at the end, or else he would have installed a luggage rack on the rear fender of his 1962 full dresser. Other than that, not much else could be added.

These two, about to make an excursion, are still young, but give them time . . . First, they'll enjoy a pleasant day of riding in the country.

A 1964 Panhead with external oil lines to the heads and twin breaker ignition.

A 1964 police model, built on the basis of the big twin Panhead. The police bikes had lower compression, additional instruments and external oil lines.

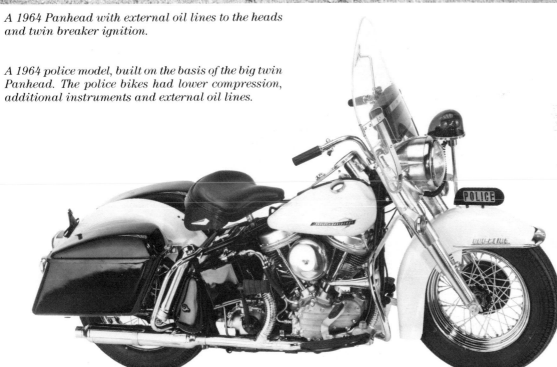

AGAIN—OUT FRONT—FOREMOST AND FIRST...

Harley-Davidson—top performer in 1956 racing!

3RD CONSECUTIVE YEAR
LEADER "GRAND NATIONAL CHAMPION" POINT STANDINGS

JOE LEONARD, FIRST; BRAD ANDRES, SECOND; EVERETT BRASHEAR, FOURTH (tie); CHARLIE WEST, FIFTH (tie); BARRY BEBB, SIXTH.

Once again, Harley-Davidson is *out front* in the Grand National Champion point standings . . . leading all other makes combined by over 30 points . . . winning all track Nationals, plus the Jack Pine, and all racing Classics! Here's a record that's tough to equal . . . set by *the* brand that's tough to beat!

These tremendous victories, in all types of competition, are your guarantee that you ride the *finest* when you ride Harley-Davidson . . . *finest* in performance, stamina and handling ease — with dynamic power to keep you foremost and first, always!

Take a tip from America's *top performing* road and track stars — ride Harley-Davidson in '57. Stop in soon for a test-ride-thrill at your Harley-Davidson dealer. Look ahead — be ahead in 1957.

3RD CONSECUTIVE YEAR
LEADER IN 1956 NATIONAL CHAMPIONSHIP PARADE

10-MILE NATIONAL ½-mile track —
Everett Brashear, Columbus, Ohio, June 10.
Time: 9 minutes, 40.10 seconds.

100-MILE NATIONAL 1-mile road course —
Brad Andres, Laconia, N.H., June 17.
Time: 1 hour, 43 minutes, 5.36 seconds.

20-MILE NATIONAL 1-mile track —
Joe Leonard, Bay Meadows, Calif., August 26.
Time: 17 minutes, 2.62 seconds.

500-MILE NATIONAL Jack Pine Endurance Run — Leroy Winters, Lansing, Mich., September 2-3. 953 points.

45° TT NATIONAL ½-mile course —
Brad Andres, Peoria, Ill., September 9.
Time: 7 minutes, 19.70 seconds.

80° TT NATIONAL ½-mile course —
Joe Leonard, Peoria, Ill., September 9.
Time: 7 minutes, 16.80 seconds.

LEADER IN AMERICA'S 1956 "CLASSIC RACES"

200-MILE CLASSIC Beach-Road Race —
John Gibson, Daytona Beach, Fla., March 11.
Time: 2 hours, 6 minutes, 21.51 seconds.

50-MILE CLASSIC ⅝-mile road course —
Brad Andres, Altoona, Pa., July 22.
Time: 1 hour, 54 seconds.

5-MILE CLASSIC ½-mile track —
Charlie West, Sturgis, S.D., August 12.
Time: 3 minutes, 03.9 seconds.

25-MILE CLASSIC 1-mile track —
Everett Brashear, Springfield, Ill., August 20.
Time: 17 minutes, 34.90 seconds.

5-MILE, 12 STAR CLASSIC ½-mile track —
Carroll Resweber, St. Paul, Minn., September 1.
Time: 4 minutes, 35.63 seconds.

100-MILE CLASSIC 1-mile speedway —
Everett Brashear, Langhorne, Pa., September 3.
Time: 1 hour, 9 minutes, 30.87 seconds.

100-MILE GRAND PRIX CLASSIC 1½-mile road course —
Bill Meier, Dodge City, Kan., September 3. Time: 1 hour, 26 minutes, 35.56 seconds.

HARLEY-DAVIDSON MOTOR CO.,
Milwaukee 1, Wisconsin

Bill Meier

Charlie West

Barry Bebb

Carroll Resweber

Brad Andres

Joe Leonard

Everett

John Gibson

Leroy Winters

142

Chapter 8

Best of the side-valves: the rapid KR

After thirty-seven years at Harley-Davidson, first as Ottaway's number two man, then as racing director, Hank Syvertsen retired in 1957. He was replaced by Dick O'Brien, who headed the racing department from 1957 to 1983, sometimes tyrannically I'm told, but almost always successfully.

After the war, Nortons, Triumphs and BSAs achieved outstanding victories and placings in diverse disciplines. All told, however, Harley-Davidson, as a single marque, still collected more trophies and laurels. The plant never hid that fact; quite the contrary. In all likelihood, the hot-selling British makers, who sold more in the United States than in all other markets combined, did not appreciate this. They complained about the decades-old Class C rules with increasing volume.

In their company publications, in the cycling press (which appreciated their ad business) as well as within the AMA, which was increasingly under their influence, the importers addressed this alleged unfairness. They claimed that the AMA was dominated by Harley-Davidson, and that it manipulated the rules to prevent Harley-Davidson's long-overdue downfall. The importers were happy to demonstrate how many victories they might have had under "normal circumstances," and sowed the suspicion that their strongest rival in the United States was too weak. The British gained the sympathy of many fans, and increased their influence within the AMA.

Today, with many years of hindsight, this campaign might appear threadbare and insidious. For one thing, the side-valve/overhead-valve rules might well appear justified. Several 500 cc machines, in the hands of careful tuners, developed higher power than the side-valve Harleys. On top of that, they were decidedly lighter. By 1968, it was well known that the British did not spend nearly as much time, effort or money on the development of their 500 cc ohv engines as their American opponents. They never utilized their design possibilities as thoroughly as the industrious Harley-Davidson racing department which, year after year, worked on their side-valve engines with ambition, devotion and sweat of brow. The Harley-Davidson side-valve racers were faster because there were people in Milwaukee who were prepared to spend the effort to keep them that way.

If we accept the premise that the British firms were, from the start, unprepared to fully develop their ohv engines because of the displacement restrictions, yet another question is raised. Several British firms had side-valve engines in their product line-ups. Why then did the

As successor to the WR models, the KR entered the Class C arena in 1952. The KR racers were derived from the new K models, and possessed the same 45 ci engine-transmission unit, four-speed foot shift and front telescoping fork. Although they soon won races, they were considered a bit lamer than the WRs.

Among the KRs, the KRTT was the road-racing version, almost always equipped with the sprung rear suspension as well as the big front brake. In comparison to the dirt-track KR, the sprung swing arm can be removed and replaced by a rigid member.

British, long dominating the US as well as the world market, and therefore hauling in healthy profits, refuse to develop their own 750 cc side-valve racers for the United States, by far their most important export market?

By the end of 1968, the time was finally ripe; under pressure from British importers, the AMA extensively changed the rules of diverse Grand National Championships. For dirt trackers, for example, rear brakes became permissible. The most dramatic change, however, was that side-valve racing machines no longer had a displacement advantage over ohv engines, which had an inherent power advantage. Further, they managed to force through a rule that racers had to be derived from production motorcycles and had to be built and sold in a limited series of at least 200 machines.

Simply put, this meant that they hoped to save themselves further design work. From the outset, their new three-cylinders had an inherent competition advantage. In view of the rapid pace of the rules changes (they were announced in November 1968, effective January 1969, and the season started in March at the latest) the importers figured on record sales of the three-cylinder machines as the basis of production racers for countless private riders. They would have to convert from their apparently weaker production KRs to the allegedly superior British racers. Furthermore, it was assumed that several of the 200 Harley works racers would certainly fall into the hands of the competition, which would then have easy access to Harley-Davidson's state of the art as well as their pioneering side-valve developments and all that followed.

O'Brien was surprised by this development and initially had nothing up his sleeve. The otherwise ignored 883 cc XLR production racer with tuned Sportster engine quickly had to be pressed into service for the new generation of racing machines. To meet the 750 cc limit, the stroke was reduced. Time was too short, and initial power output was hardly more than the fully developed side-valve racers, and it was more fragile.

At the important season opener, the 200 miler on the Daytona long course, BSA, Norton and Triumph showed up with their new 750 cc ohv machines. Several riders on the works Harley-Davidson team started on KRTTs, then developing over 60 hp. In front of press, public, betting parlors and the competition, the British triples and twins, the Japanese 500s, even the 350 two-strokes had already shown their stuff in earlier races. The first motorcycle to cross the finish line was Cal Rayborn's KRTT, with an incredible one-and-a-half lap lead. A more poignant comment to the eternal side-valve/over-head-valve quarrels could hardly be possible. What a noble exit for Harley-Davidson's last side-valve racing machine!

In the next year, Honda of America announced racing versions of their 750 cc four-cylinder machines; Yamaha, Kawasaki and Suzuki started with reworked two-stroke rockets. The era of the classic Harley-Davidson street racers was nearly over. The Italian Harley-Davidson subsidiary, Aermacchi, would for a time displace the Japanese competition and their two-strokes from the victor's podium. But the epoch of British bikes, too, was nearing its end.

The KRM of 1954, intended for the long-distance desert races of California, in which British makes were becoming too pushy for Milwaukee's tastes. But weighing 45 pounds more than the competition, the KRM was neither a sporting nor a sales success.

KR of 1955.

Carroll Resweber in September 1959. Only Jay Springsteen, at a much later time, would similarly dominate the sport. In 1958, 1959, 1960 and 1961, he was champion, far ahead of the rest. In 1962 he was second to the fast-climbing Bart Markel. Today, Resweber is a tuner and manager of a sponsored XR team in the Camel Pro series.

"Bad" Bart Merkel of Flint, Michigan, was for a long time one of the top national riders, winning the hard-fought title of Grand National Champion in 1962, 1965 and 1966.

148

The road-racing KRTT of 1966.

A still from the motorcycle racing movie On Any Sunday *of 1972. Hitting the dirt is Cal Rayborn. About to hit the dirt is Mark Brelsford.*

Whether or not Roger Reiman came out of this incredible broadslide is not known. His overwhelm-ing success is probably due to this style, which doesn't even let his pursuers appear in the same photo.

Chapter 9

Sportster — Harley's hammer

How does one begin the story of the Sportster, the "other" V-twin classic from Milwaukee? It was of the same flesh and blood as the KH models, built from 1954 to the present day, which in turn were born of the K models, in the program since 1952. The design department led by William J. Harley (son of the first chief designer) built upon the basic KH exactly that which I had speculated at the beginning of the Knucklehead chapter. Harley-Davidson had already tried something like it on the old flathead: they removed the valves from a side-valve engine, gave it pushrods and replaced the old head with a new ohv model.

That not only worked, but also turned the weak-selling KH into the best seller of the following year, the dream of every all-American (and non-American) boy: the exuberant, brutal Sportster, capable of leaving anything on two wheels and most things on four wheels in its dust. In 1957, the Sportster was exactly the right answer to the British bikes. No engine from Albion could keep up with it, yet with only 55 ci, 883 cc, it stayed under the sensitive American insurance limit for 900 cc bikes, which separated "expensive" from "too expensive."

Granted, the cut-down XL could not compare with the refined suspensions of the Norton or Triumph. If racing on a curved road, the Brits might be able to make up in the turns what they lacked on the straights, but as soon as the road was clear, these troublesome competitors were soon left behind. The Sportster was simply untouchable in acceleration, torque and top speed.

This lasted one whole year. Then the Sportster, dubbed XLH after 1958, was left behind by a still faster Sportster, the XLCH. This was a trimmed-down competition version, onto which many speed freaks simply bolted a headlamp to make it street legal, and proceeded to blow away not only the Brits, but also the XLHs. Milwaukee took note; starting in 1959, the XLCH was delivered in street-legal form. One model year later, the high pipes were replaced by low dual staggered pipes.

The XLH had the larger tank, battery ignition and was tuned a bit softer. In 1965 it got twelve volts to replace the six-volt system, and an electric starter followed in 1967. The XLCH had the smaller peanut tank and magneto ignition, which was replaced by battery ignition in 1969. In character, the XLCH was rough, but the XLH could not by any means be considered soft. Regardless, both coexisted happily for a long time; the XLCH sold better than the XLH. At the end of the 1960s, the British bikes could finally match their power. But by that time, the Japanese Honda fours and Kawasaki two-stroke threes were leaving them all behind.

Thanks to generally increased buying power, an active awareness of leisure time and reawakened interest in clean middle-class motorcycles (assisted in no small part by the outstanding ad campaigns of the Japanese), the motorcycle market exploded. Harley got a piece of the action, but most went to the Japanese.

AMF took over the last American motorcycle plant in 1969. The AMF marketing "experts" suddenly had a voice in Milwaukee's operations. The first year in which they had a say, 1970, brought the long plastic "boat tail" to the Sportster. Because every motorcycle sold better than in the previous year, 1971 saw tails attached to the new Super Glide, the mixture of big twin and Sportster. But they must have noticed something was amiss, because in 1972 the embarrassing plastic bits were left off both models.

For 1972, the engineers increased the cylinder bore of both the electric-start and kick-start Sportsters, but retained the stroke; displacement increased from 883 to just under 1000 cc. To give the machines a different appearance, many engine parts were dipped in black lacquer. Instead of the Tillotson, they installed the smaller, knee-friendly Bendix carburetor, which also provided better fueling.

A long period followed without any new developments, ending in 1977, when the XLCR was unveiled by the factory as a devilishly quick experiment from Willie G. Davidson's private workshop. If the mood struck, the average rider could use this device on Wisconsin's public roads to show the Japanese bikes (English bikes had all but disappeared) what a Harley could do. The frame improvements went into production, but the engine of the series cafe racer (XLCR) was in a considerably more civilized state of tune than Willie's own cafe rocket. Regardless, it was the fastest version of the Sportster to date, and with this machine Harley-Davidson riders could once again keep up with the fast big ones.

The gleaming black boulevard beauty was quite stunning. In the first year, almost 2,000 were sold, not a bad number. In 1978 it was only

Same procedure every day. Fuel and oil are poured into the newly assembled bike, it's put on the chassis dynamometer and all functions and gears are tested. If the new Harley-Davidson graduates, it can continue on to its existence; otherwise, it goes back to school before being tested again. This photo is from Milwaukee, but the scene in York, Pennsylvania, is not much different.

152

1,200, which hardly made the production effort worthwhile. If we are to believe the records, only nine sales contracts for cafe racers were signed in 1979.

The frame design of the XLCR was applied to the normal Sportster in 1979, which improved the handling of the XLH and the new XLS Roadster. Purists were bothered by the sight of the unusual frame as well as the siamese twin pipes. The kick-start XLCH was banished from the line-up in that year, because it was hardly different from the XLH.

After the collapse of XLCR sales, and the protests against the appearance of the 1979 Sportsters, the powers at AMF were not keen on every new idea coming from Willie G. When he presented a new 1000 cc high-speed prototype, consisting of some XLH but more importantly also XR 750 flat-track-racer parts, with lots of aluminum, two carburetors and raked exhausts, the reaction was shock: "Now what's he up to?" They asked him, in a polite way, to come to his senses.

Separation from AMF came in 1981. Willie's influence on company policy was again felt in the independent firm. To survive, the company needed to exploit specialized market segments. The XR 1000 was conceived as an expensive, special model for connoisseurs and appeared on the market in limited numbers in 1983. It's not as fast as the real competition XR 750 and not as fast as many a Japanese bike, but on no other motorcycle does one feel or, indeed, sound as fast.

For the 1983 model year, the Sportster program was extended downward with the XLX 61, again a bare-bones Sportster with only the most essential equipment. It sold well from the very beginning, and was economical—or relatively economical, as we are speaking of a Harley-Davidson. It then proceeded to win many friends with its uncluttered beauty, which recalled the first Sportster of the late fifties.

Beginning with the 1986 model year, the new Sportster appeared, with a nonisolated 55 ci, 883 cc engine hung directly in the frame. This XL 883 was soon followed by the XLH with 1100 cc. The XL had a 76.2 mm or 3 in. bore, the XLH had an 85.1 mm bore and both shared a stroke of 96.8 mm or $3^{13}/_{16}$ in. Compression was raised from 8.8:1 in the preceding series to 9:1.

Thanks to quality changes at the plant, about which we'll have more to say, mechanical noise from the engine was reduced, although these motors still have four cams, four pushrods and five speeds. A black box, dubbed V-Fire III, managed the ignition in a manner similar to the Blockhead, with vacuum advance, breakerless and electronic. Both Sportsters possessed the same suspension. The small single-seater was pointed with small handlebars, the twin-saddle model with buckhorn. The small machine could be equipped with an additional seat, extra foot-pegs and metallic paint to upgrade it to the XL De Luxe level. There remains only one difference discernible to the eye: the black cylinders of the 1100 cc.

Like all Harley-Davidson frames, that of the Sportster is electrostatically given a positive charge; in the paint booth, it attracts the negatively charged powder coat particles. The result is a thick, hard coat and one of the reasons why Harleys cost more. Despite such features, the small Sporty is the first Harley in a long time to break the $4,000 magic barrier—at $3,995.

The XL develops 46 bhp at 6000 rpm; maximum torque is 46 lb-ft at 4000 rpm. The 1100 cc XLH puts out 58 lb-ft, also at 4000, and 54 bhp in the US market. In the German market, five horses are lost to squeak under the 50 hp insurance limit.

The long-awaited successor to the familiar W model range arrived in mid-1952 as the Model K. Engine and transmission in one unit, telescoping fork at the front, swing arm at the rear, foot shift and hand clutch. Add to that the pleasing four-gallon tank and sprung solo saddle. Yet the new 750 cc side-valve, with about 30 hp and 420 lb. curb weight, wasn't enough to prevent many a rider from looking up the pipes of English bikes. For the golden anniversary year of 1954, a displacement increase to 883 cc changed it to the otherwise identical Model KH. Bore was retained, stroke increased, valves enlarged, crankshaft, clutch and transmission reworked. The KH was faster, but still left some power wishes unfulfilled.

Not so the first Sportster, the 1957 XL, an ohv version developed from the KH. Again 55 ci displacement, the original three-inch bore of the K and a stroke reduced to 3 13/16, which helped raise the rev limit. The 7.5:1 compression was unassuming for an ohv. The light alloy pushrods were driven by four case-mounted camshafts, just as the valves themselves had been driven earlier. The pushrods actuated the rocker arms, located in new rocker boxes; the rocker arms in turn actuated the valves. Combustion chambers were hemispherical, the light alloy pistons were domed. One year later the compression was raised to 9:1 and the model designation changed to XLH.

154

Stripped-down Sportster, designated XLC in its first year of 1958, later XLCH, with high-mounted exhausts and 2¼ gallon peanut tank, were also offered. Dick O'Brien's assistant in the racing department, Clyde Denzer, is using this 1961 XLCH to demonstrate that this Sportster version was quite capable of handling off-road excursions. The tires' block tread pattern made cross-country riding easier. Given seat, lighting and speedometer, the Sportster was fully street-legal. As an aside, the decorative H on the oil tank of many Harleys stood for Highway use.

This is really the 1965 XLA, a sort of full-dresser Sportster with military equipment, the last motorcycle that Harley-Davidson was able to sell to the Pentagon in significant numbers.

Another satisfied Sportster customer! Here we see Willie G. performing the routine handshake, handing over the keys and smiling at the camera at a promotional event. Whether the other three are VIPs isn't known. The XLH of 1979 took over most of the new suspension of the XLCR cafe racer, shown in the color pages. That made for a good ride, but for many potential customers, the triangular frame and siamesed exhaust looked too conventional or even too Japanese. It had to be removed from the line-up.

The XLH Sportster of 1980, the last XL model whose frame included welded, cast components.

The 1000 cc Roadster, Model XLS of 1982. This touring version of the Sportster was softer and had a larger tank, thicker saddle, wire-spoked wheels, sissy bar, two-inch-longer fork tubes and highway pegs. The new frame was easier to manufacture because cast parts were no longer welded in; if anything, the ride quality increased as a result.

The XLX-61, in 1983 the lowest-priced Harley, but with a price of $3,995. Customers asked themselves why a few dollars were saved on the second saddle and rear footpegs. To move the otherwise popular XLX, the dealers usually installed these themselves, even though the profit margin on this machine was slim. Some details were irritating, such as the speedometer cable routed over the headlamp. If not installed properly, the heat shield of the rear exhaust contacted against the brake cylinder cover and could rub through.

From the left side, too, the XR 1000 of 1984 was impressive. The most potent street Harley, a mean machine borne of the XL and XR 750, it served as the base machine for the Battle of the Twins road races. The exhaust ports are forward pointing, just as on the XR dirt-track bikes; the two Dell'Orto carburetors are angled to the rear; the heavy cast-iron cylinders are topped by aluminum heads. The machine was difficult to hold above about 110 mph; at the present writing I know of no one who has given the bike its head. In West Germany this bike has no general service permit, and must be individually certified.

In 1986, the German Harley-Davidson display included this prototype built on a Sportster basis. The object was to test public reaction and interest to a restyled XL variant. The chief of the US export organization, Len Thompson, commissioned the German designer Hans Muth to perform this study. Muth had previously gained attention with his Suzuki Katana, so it's no surprise that this machine looks familiar. The assignment was mainly to restyle the tank and saddle. I personally like the two exhaust pipes. I'm eager to see if the German designer, Luigi Colani, is available and affordable.

Evolution Sportster, 883 cc. To round out the rather complete collection of Sportsters, beginning with the 1987 models the cylinder head casting method was changed and the combustion chamber shape was altered to resemble that of the XR 750. Crankshaft main and connecting rod bearings were given steel cages for better heat resistance, the gear ratios were more closely spaced and the distributor advance was recurved.

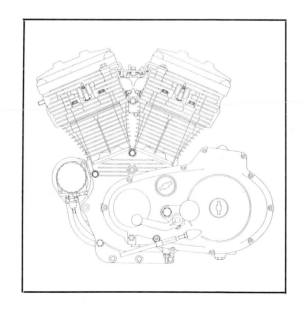

The distinctly better-equipped XLH of 1988, with 1200 cc motor.

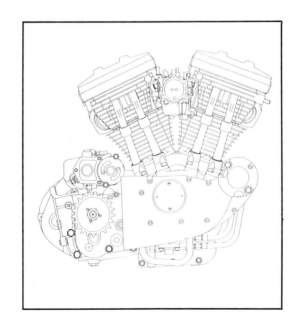

Founded in Los Angeles in 1935, the McLaglen Motorcycle Corps drill team traveled throughout the country with the well-known actor's troupe. Their competition in the Rose Bowl in 1936 has become legend; there, before 60,000 spectators, they competed against the Mexico City Police Stunt Team, also on Harleys. After hours of the most astounding demonstrations, the American team won by a small margin. The current president is an undertaker; among other things, his team escorts "De Luxe" funeral processions. A pity that the deceased can't share the experience.

FLH 74, model year 1977, with Keihin carburetor, new sprung saddle, the small Tour Pak and standard anti-theft alarm.

The 61 ci Sportster XL of 1976.

The Electra Glide Classic of 1979 (FLH 80) with King Tour Pak. After mid-1980, the FLHs were available only with the larger motor and the toaster air filter. The new seats of the 1979 were roomier and generally more comfortable than the previous sprung saddle, which was still available. The long exhaust pipes hang up on curbs.

In Monza, Italy, 1973, the two factory riders Renzo Pasolini and Walter Villa were involved in a tragic accident at the start. Pasolini was killed, Villa was seriously injured. Aboard Harley-Davidson/Aermacchi's fantastically quick water-cooled two-strokes, Villa won the 250 cc road-racing championships of 1974, 1975 and 1976, and also the 1976 350 championship. This proved the abilities of the Italian engineers, and how greatly the motorcycle philosophies of parent company and subsidiary differed.

Today a collector piece, the combination of drag racer, Sportster and boulevard cruiser parts that combine to make the cafe racer XLCR.

This is why I've always looked forward to the press previews of new Harleys. With the Fat Bob (left) as well as the Super Glide, you could go like hell, or instantly behave like a solid citizen. After 1979, both were available with the 80 ci powerplant, with the 1200 cc optional. The name Fat Bob comes from the West Coast custom scene. A Harley stripped to the bare essentials was "bobbed"; if instead of a peanut tank the "fat" two-part standard tank was then installed, it became a Fat Bob.

In 1979, the great Jay Springsteen was still winning motocross-like stadium TTs with his XR 750 at a time when victory rostrums were already being filled by riders of Japanese machinery. 1979.

The magnificent seven, Harley-Davidson's racing elite. Three Grand National champions, from left: Scott Parker, Randy Goss, Jay Springsteen; in the center, tuner Brent Thomsen; in front an aluminum XR, and then three Harley-Davidson racing managers, Bill Werner, the present boss, Dick O'Brien, who had the job for over 20 years, and his former number two and successor, Clyde Denzer, Werner's predecessor.

Those were the days: L.A. Custom Show, 1980. A Shovelhead chopper, southern California style. The fork is so long, it had to go on the next slide.

The 1980 Tour Glide. With improved suspension, engine and transmission mounted on isolators, five-speed transmission, oil-bath secondary chain, one-piece tank and instruments mounted on the steering head, undoubtedly a better bike than the Electra Glide, but is it a better Harley?

The FXWG Wide Glide, one of the finest factory choppers, in its first model year, 1980. Displacement of 1340 cc, widened and lengthened fork, lidless Sportster headlamp, risers with buckhorn bars, 21 inch front wheel, forward-mounted foot levers, flamed split five-gallon tank, staggered shorty duals, stepped seat, shortened rear shocks and typical rear fender.

The 1982 FXB Sturgis with primary as well as secondary belt drive. The belt inside the primary housing was a pain to remove, but in between overhauls held up well. Secondary drive by belt has since become widely accepted at Harley-Davidson.

The Dragons of Berlin ride out. The $50,000 that the Berlin police had to pay to the club for illegal seizure of and damage to their Harleys made headlines all over Germany. Franki (center), president of the MC Dragons, hopes that the authorities will now be a bit more circumspect when dealing with the motorcycle clubs. The astounded German taxpayers will probably share that sentiment.

The Disc Glide, a Wide Glide variant of 1984 with rear disc wheel and secondary belt drive, was never offered for sale in West Germany. A modern classic from the collection of Paul Watts.

Sometimes you wish for more knowledge in your head and more hardware in the parts bin. Summer vacation, 1986, with my 80 ci 1980 FLH dresser.

Chapter 10

The Shovelhead generation

In the gentleman's club atmosphere of the AMA governing body, concerns about the Japanese invasion did not enter the minds of the functionaries, importers, Harley managers, dealers and members of the press. After all, cheap mini-bikes were not to be compared with their heavy, quality motorcycles. The Japanese should try to build a proper motorcycle! What could possibly happen? Everybody knew that the American market for motorized two-wheelers would never exceed 100,000 per year. It had been so for decades.

The management of the Harley-Davidson Motor Company really did concern itself with this easily surveyed market. With the two-stroke 125 cc Hummer, the 175 cc Bobcat, Ranger, Pacer and Scat (its successors from 1962 onward), the pleasing little Topper motorscooter, the 250 and 350 cc four-stroke singles from Aermacchi, the fast 883 cc Sportsters as well as the 1200 cc big twins, which could be equipped according to the gusto of the buyer, the firm offered an attractive, well-rounded program in all but the 500 to 750 cc class.

Harley-Davidson's designers generally developed their detail improvements at a leisurely pace, adding this refinement, deleting that. In the fall of 1965 they made another great leap forward and presented their big twins for 1966. The new cylinder head was immediately obvious. Instead of shrouding the rockers as had been the practice on the Panhead, they were now integrated in the new rocker box. The generator remained at the front of the crankcase. Fuel was metered by a Tillotson membrane carburetor. And that was about all in the way of engine changes.

Better electrics, the added touring package consisting of police windscreen and fiberglass bags made the complete motorcycle heavier. The new FLH was listed at 60 hp—barely ten percent more power. But thanks to its weight, the first Shovelheads were a bit slower than the last Panheads. The lower-compression FL put out 54 hp, but was never as popular as the FLH. Most FLs were ordered by police and government agencies. The wonderful tourers and dressers, which could be assembled from the impressive Harley accessory catalog, had no equals anywhere in the world, and today still overshadow the later efforts of the competition.

The magazines criticized the brakes, in need of improvement, and also the fact that the good looking suspended double saddle was too short and located too far forward, so that on long runs, the passenger pushed the rider too far

The first Electra Glide with Shovelhead motor appeared in 1966. This FLH has the complete touring package: police screen, spotlights, blinkers, saddlebags, case guards, luggage rack, fender trim, De Luxe saddle, fishtail exhaust and stovepipe around the front exhaust manifold. Now you know why it needed the big 12-volt battery, hidden behind its chrome covers.

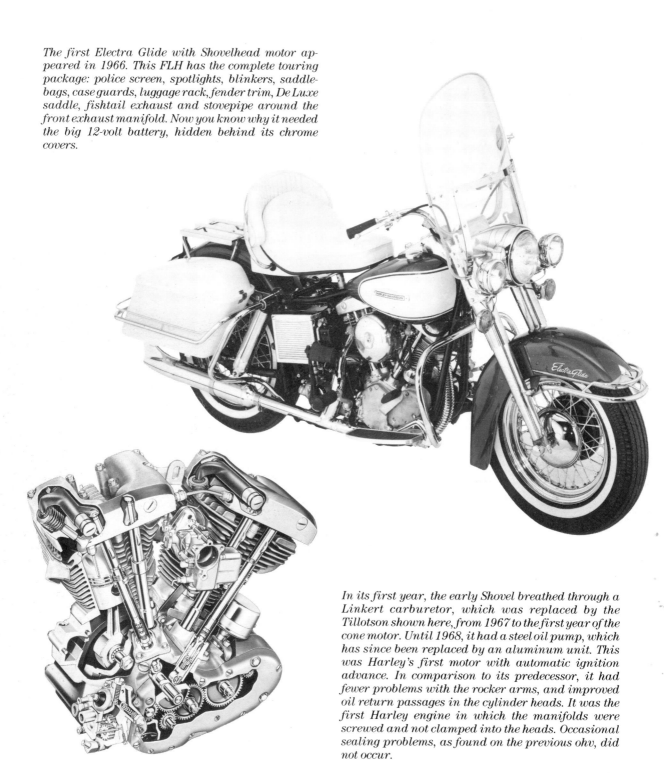

In its first year, the early Shovel breathed through a Linkert carburetor, which was replaced by the Tillotson shown here, from 1967 to the first year of the cone motor. Until 1968, it had a steel oil pump, which has since been replaced by an aluminum unit. This was Harley's first motor with automatic ignition advance. In comparison to its predecessor, it had fewer problems with the rocker arms, and improved oil return passages in the cylinder heads. It was the first Harley engine in which the manifolds were screwed and not clamped into the heads. Occasional sealing problems, as found on the previous ohv, did not occur.

forward. The solo version, however, with its comfortable police saddle, lower vibration level and outstanding overall impression was praised by reviewers.

Up to 1970, we are talking about the "early Shovel" or "generator Shovel," thereafter the "cone" or simply the Shovel motor. The front-mounted generator was replaced by the generator mounted at the top of the primary drive housing. The ignition advance was shifted to the cone on the right side of the crankcase. The kick starter was eliminated. In 1971 the Tillotson was replaced by the Bendix carburetor, which in turn was followed by the Keihin in 1974. The new front disc brake of 1972 was said to produce good braking action. I don't know what happened to the disc or why they didn't keep it in succeeding years because it's hard to believe that an FLH could brake well.

Apparently, somebody in Milwaukee was reading the motorcycle tests of the preceding ten or fifteen years, because in 1973 the sprung

From 1969 onward, the Electra Glide spread its wings. Yet another functional classic which, after nearly 30 years, has lost nothing of its appeal. What other motorcycle could stand beside it and even remotely satisfy your desire for beauty? With my brother in the north end of Frankfurt, West Germany, sometime in the 1970s.

The Harley-Davidson alarm clock. What company has ever brought out a nicer speedometer?

The 1971 Super Glide showed that the company took the new generation of customers seriously, for whom the expansive E-Glides were too big, and the Sportsters too hard. Willie G. says that the FX design was finalized in 1967, but found little interest in pre-AMF days. The company leadership felt that it had the youth market covered with the Sportster. At AMF the idea finally got through. The Sportster front end and 19 inch wheel was attached to a stripped FLH frame, with big twin motor and without the electric starter. The result was the Super Glide. The tail stayed for only a year, while the split tank and siamesed exhaust lived for two years. Its combined handle FX, made up from FLH and XLH, indicates its parentage.

saddle was extended and divided. In the next year, even the license plate frame was equipped with an alarm. As far as I'm concerned, they might well bring that back in an improved form, as it would simplify many a short outing. Finally, in 1978, the breakerless electronic ignition was installed in a small black can at the front. In the event of problems, this item could only be tossed and replaced by a new unit.

With the increasingly stringent noise and emissions standards of Western nations, which paid scant attention to the huge, loud, stinking diesels but directed much of their efforts to the small, voiceless minority of motorcyclists, decibel levels were lowered every year or exhaust gas was further filtered. I wouldn't want to inhale from the ends of the exhaust pipes in order to make a direct comparison of the qualitative improvements in the exhaust emissions of a '78 compared to a '73. The difference won't be all that great; I'm hard pressed to detect the difference in noise level. In any case, the regulatory restraints did little to protect lungs or nerves, but the beefy character of Harleys suffered regardless. To compensate, from 1978 onward, an 80 ci engine was offered in addition to the 74 ci. This engine breathed through a large toaster air filter without losing power. After 1980, only the larger 1340 cc engine was available.

There follows a brief history lesson. After that, we can look at the pictures, with which, assisted by captions, we examine in detail the creations of one William G. Davidson, which gradually entered the program beginning in 1971, creations such as the Super Glide, Fat Bob, Low Rider, Wide Glide, Disc Glide, Sturgis.

The FX soon stood on its own feet. For 1973, it appealed to buyers with its Italo-Harley-Sprint-inspired bread-loaf tank and shorty duals. From 1974, there was also an FXE available, E for electric starter. With that, even those who had problems with kick-starters could join the fun. The FXE became more popular; both models changed little over the years, if we disregard the exhausts and other minor details. In 1977 the frame changed slightly, but that year brought an important surprise . . .

. . . that surprise was the introduction of the black-and-silver FXS Low Rider for the 1978 sales year. The FXS was intended to strengthen the bond between the factory and the custom scene. The Low Rider was Milwaukee's first all-around aesthetically pleasing factory custom. Principally an FXE with shortened fork and springs, a broader spread to the fork stanchion tubes, increased wheelbase, drag bars on risers, a new instrument panel atop the Fat Bob tank, polished upper cooling fins and ample crinkle-finish lacquer. At about the same time as the FXS's appearance, the custom segment in places far removed from the home market developed an appetite for increasingly powerful Japanese bikes with less character, against whom Harley-Davidson could not and would not compete.

174

As the American Machine and Foundry Corporation (AMF) took over Harley-Davidson in 1969, one important part of the deal was that the production facilities of the motorcycle plant were to be modernized. But first, AMF increased the production figures. Output climbed to 75,000 units per year. As a result, the aging plant as well as the second- and third-generation Harley craftsmen were simply overtaxed. The build quality of the machines delivered to dealers was clearly dropping and eventually reached scandalous levels. This was really not the right recipe for success against the wide-awake Japanese competition, which had meanwhile set new standards for quality and affordability. Despite the increasing production figures, attained under pressure, Harley's portion of the booming motorcycle market fell year after year; Harley had not had an overwhelming share of the market, and now could not even maintain that small percentage.

Furthermore, AMF leadership had a hierarchical policy; to those who had to actually carry them out, many decisions from the highest levels seemed totally ill-considered or even against their interests. The previously almost familiar relationship between the old management and its employees became clouded; both organized

Early August 1979: Along with thousands of others astride their large-displacement V-twins, Willie G. and Louis Netz rode their pre-production FXBs to the South Dakota hills for the Sturgis rally, just to chew the fat, have some fun and admire some good-looking machines. The mills ridden by the two Harley designers, so similar to the Low Riders, had the 80 ci motor, the joined Super Glide exhaust and the nice drag bars, like those that Dennis Hopper held so dear in Easy Rider. *The B in FXB stood for belt, as in primary and secondary drive belts. Harley developed these in association with the Gates Rubber Company. Belt drive itself was no great achievement; belts generally lasted 30,000 maintenance-free miles. The problem lay in finding room for the belt. In the following model years, the FXB, nicknamed Sturgis, breathed through shorty duals, and buckhorns unfortunately replaced the drag bars.*

175

and wildcat strikes as well as work stoppages came about, and there was even talk of sabotage. Regularly scheduled layoffs added fuel to the fire.

In its own way, AMF kept its promise to modernize the plant. Instead of carrying this through in Milwaukee, with experienced Harley builders, only the company headquarters as well as engine, transmission and drive manufacture remained there and were overhauled. AMF management, disgusted with its stubborn Milwaukee employees, shifted all other jobs as well as final assembly to the faraway town of York, Pennsylvania.

The new factory choppers and customs sold better than the E-Glide. Beginning with the company's 75th anniversary, in 1978, the FLH could be ordered with the 1200 cc or larger 80 ci motor with larger air filter. The two cylinders, giving 1340 cc, could hardly push the E-Glide faster than the classic 74 ci twin. A limited Classic series of fully equipped creme and tan FLHs, with the big motor and choice of sprung or rigid saddle, followed in 1979.

176

A quality control problem was painfully obvious with the FLHC Classic or Heritage model of 1981—unbalanced crankshafts. The resulting shivering gradually distributed parts of the motorcycle along the road. The heavy E-Glide further suffered from the annual tightening of noise and emissions limits. These were difficult to achieve with an antique, air-cooled V-twin developing acceptable power. Meeting the limits was keeping more than two thirds of the Harley designers busy. As a way out, the big twin motor was generally delivered in its 1340 cc form.

Black is beautiful, and the Low Rider of 1981 was even blacker than before. In an interview, Willie G. said the low rider concept was born at custom meets of the early seventies. The trends that developed there, and from conversations with bikers, were blended with his own ideas. At today's meets, the "G-man" still seems inquisitive, looks closely, asks questions and listens carefully to the explanations.

There, the company had an underutilized munitions factory, which was overhauled to the tune of several million dollars. Workers were recruited from the local labor pool, which at that time were not exactly the cream of America's metalworker crop. With that, the quality problems were far from solved. Add to that the unforeseen jump in transport costs between Milwaukee and York, thanks to the energy crisis. To top it all off, there was the long, difficult strike in Milwaukee in 1974. A year later both plants went on strike, which brought the company to a standstill for months on end and robbed it of the much-needed profits from four whole months of motorcycles which were never built.

The FXDG Disc Glide, seen from the right. In the color section, Paul Watts' FXDG is seen from the left, revealing its drive; here you can see the timing side. The FXDG of 1984 was an FXWG Wide Glide equipped with disc wheel, belt drive and bags. The flame tank FXWG Original appeared in 1980. The Wide Glide took the custom concept one step further and was the first real factory chopper; one of the rolling sculptures which made its designers, Willie G. and Lou Netz, popular.

In the 1970s, the important large tourer market, previously the absolute domain of the E-Glide and a few BMWs, was being increasingly taken over by the Honda Gold Wing and other Japanese cruisers. Harley-Davidson was dependent on continued sales to the tourer market and was able to bring out a significant new model in 1980, the FLT Tour Glide. A thoroughly thought out travel machine with components harmonized to each other, it brought back a good part of the target buyers. The motor, mounted in rubber isolators, transmitted less vibration to the rider. The five-speed transmission needed even less revs in daily use than previously. The secondary drive chain ran in a sealed oil bath. The new suspension allowed these new bikes to move more easily at low speed and in curves. Here an FLTC, Tour Glide Classic of 1981.

179

Going through them changes: the 1981 Super Glide got a bigger brake anchor at the rear, as well as more durable batteries. The Shovel of the time prompted the question, Can't you hear me knockin'?, which the factory answered with lower compression of 7.4:1 for the 80 ci motor. In its final year, 1983, the FXE was the lowest-cost version of the big bikes. It had double disc brakes at the front, but no kick-starter, no double tank, no sissy bar and a cheaper exhaust.

The 1982 Super Glide was still available alongside its successors. Because the replacement machine had a completely different look, the FXR has since been called the Super Glide II. The II was given the Tour Glide frame and the rubber-isolated 80 ci Shovel motor, as well as the five-speed transmission. The top model shown here, the FXRS version of the standard FXR, had a two-tone paint job and more complete equipment. Many buyers liked the noticeable improvements, but the chopper builders grumbled about the frame.

What would they have said about this one? After the success of the FLT, the marketing strategists smelled blood. From 1983 onward, they wanted to win back an even greater share of the touring market with the FXRT Sport Glide, based on the police version FXRP. Riding the FXRT, I was impressed by one masterpiece of the development engineers, a piece which must surely shame the Japanese competition: the relatively simple function of the gas-pressurized anti-dive front fork. Other than that, my reaction was the same as that of many potential customers who preferred the traditional styling of the E and Tour Glides. The FXRT was removed from the program at the end of 1987.

A German-market version of the E-Glide, with police screen, the outstanding Flex Seat, which allows saddle height adjustment, and wire-spoke wheels. Vaughn Beals and his wife chose this beautiful machine for a European vacation, after whose rain-soaked end the bike and riders rested in Stuttgart, West Germany, and Vaughn had to spend some time in the hospital.

The last traditional E-Glide of the old school, with belt drive, standard frame mount seat and, after 1982, new grips.

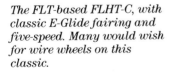

The FLT-based FLHT-C, with classic E-Glide fairing and five-speed. Many would wish for wire wheels on this classic.

In the years of overlapping model lines, special models such as this rudimentary FLHS E-Glide of 1983 always found favor with customers. Other than case guards, I wouldn't add a thing. The repairable wire wheels, the classic alarm clock atop the tank, battery and bags without covers, a right-side-only dual exhaust and deep comfort saddle. Why was this available only in the seventies?

Now then, finally, the very last of the Mohicans. The last Shovelheads left the assembly line in June 1984, and were still offered in the 1985 model year. The special edition of the FLHS seems to be the proper conclusion to the 18 year presence of these fine motors and frames. Both Shovel themes were once again united in the FLHS. From the E-Glide: headlamp, fork and fender, and 16 inch wheels. From the Wide Glide: handlebars, highway pegs instead of floorboards, chopper brake and shift levers, shorty dual exhausts and wire-spoke wheels. There's no reason to be sentimental at the parting; Shovelheads will be with us for a long time, as classics, just like the Knuckleheads and Panheads from which they developed.

The Wild One *really has motorcycle scenes only at the very beginning. In the movie, Marlon Brando rode a Triumph. In real life he knew better, and rode Harleys. He dominates the picture as troubled, mumbling gang leader Johnny. Thanks to his intro- verted confusion, he doesn't notice that Mary Murphy, the leading lady, is lame. Thankfully, Lee Marvin enters, roaring drunk, laughing, accompanied by his boys—most of them on Harleys. The film was banned in Britain for 14 years.*

As soon as Elvis Presley could afford it, he got his first
Harley—a KH. He then ordered the latest big twins
and Sportsters at yearly intervals. Many were
personally picked up in Milwaukee. The King did not
skimp on accessories, as we can see in the second
photo.

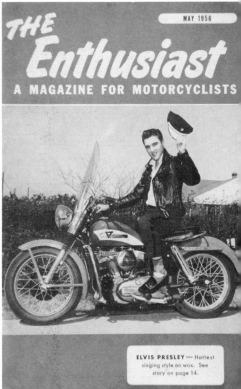

MAY 1956

THE Enthusiast
A MAGAZINE FOR MOTORCYCLISTS

ELVIS PRESLEY — Hottest
singing style on wax. See
story on page 14.

In 1966, Brigitte Bardot had her friend Serge Gainsbourg wrote a song about what her chopped 45 ci Harley-Davidson meant to her: "Je n'ai pas besoin personne au Harley-Davidson." Roughly translated, "I don't need anybody on my Harley-Davidson." She and Gainsbourg are said to have enjoyed rides on his big twins.

In the 1930s, the Enthusiast mentioned a friendly motorcycle club, the Hell's Angels. That club ceased to exist long before the name was made internationally known by a wild group from the California postwar generation. The famous or rather infamous Hell's Angels Sonny Barger, Terry the Tramp, Skip, Tiny, Magoo and others from Oakland, California, played themselves in the film Hell's Angels '69. They apparently did so convincingly; in spite of weaknesses in the script, it's considered one of the better road movies. Here an Angel is trying to move a few potentially tender steaks to the barbecue pit.

As a quick moneymaker, in 1966 Roger Corman brought out Wild Angels, *the first of many outlaw movies. Peter Fonda as Blues is tolerable, Bruce Dern is better as Loser. Why Nancy Sinatra sold her (and her father's) name for 30,000 pieces of silver remains Corman's marketing secret. The story steers toward a drawn-out conclusion, in which the group lays out the dead Loser in a small town's chapel and forces the preacher to perform the service. As he does so, the rowdies are bored by his words, preferring instead to have an orgy in the chapel. The bewildered minister escapes, and, no less bewildered, looks at their unique choppers. With them, the outlaws then bring Loser to the town cemetery, where enraged citizens try to teach them some morals. As the police arrive, the bikers take off. Only Loser and Blues stay behind, one because he's too dead, the other because he's too dumb or noble to run. The film was a box office hit; not only that, it was chosen as the official American entry at the Venice Film Festival, which (difficult as it may be to believe) it won. Personally, I would rather see a Corman film than a Godard or a Bergman.*

After Mardi Gras. Billy (Dennis Hopper), dying, just before Wyatt (Peter Fonda) gets blown away. Joe Teresi, Easyriders publisher and artful dodger, in the final act of his motorcycle rodeo, has riders playing Billy and Captain America roll into the arena, followed by a pickup driven by the rednecks. They bring the bikers down, but this time the good guys are on the ball and knock off their would-be murderers first. The crowd, often numbering in the tens of thousands, cheers, the two protagonists plant giant American and Easyriders flags on the sissy bars of their bikes, and make one more lap of the field to wild applause.

Captain America, Peter Fonda. Easy Rider *is a biker movie that actually tells more about the United States of its time than about Panhead choppers, and precisely for that reason, makes them all the more interesting. Its director, writer and star Dennis Hopper and star Peter Fonda identified themselves with their theme, and had a sufficiently artistic format to tell a believable story for the younger generation.*

In the postwar market, it was difficult to compete with the well-received British bikes. Indian tried the parallel twin design and succeeded in breaking its own neck, because they did not have the everyday reliability of the British machines. In Milwaukee, deliberations were a bit more thorough, and immediately concentrated on the more open market for small motorcycles. Here, at the 1948 introduction of the first Harley-Davidson two-stroke, are Gordon Davidson, William Harley, Jr., Arthur Davidson and William H. Davidson, from left.

Basically, the 125 cc two-stroke Harleys were copied German DKWs. As a result of the war, the victors could save development costs and licensing fees. These bikes became popular as a second bike, for hobby or utility purposes and for younger riders. The factory also offered an accessory range for these. Technically, they were steadily improved: telescoping fork (yes, it was then called Tele-Glide!), displacement increases, rear suspension and off-road version.

189

In 1960 Harley-Davidson president William H. Davidson assumed majority interest in Aermacchi and took on the Italian machines (175, 250 and later 350 ohv singles) as complements to the Harley sales program. The scrambler, shown here, was a marketing success, developing 25 hp at 8700 rpm, an incredible speed for a pushrod engine. The scrambler was given a 350 cc engine in 1972, but by that time, due to price and quality control problems, it was experiencing rough going in the marketplace against the Japanese.

The so-called Nova, co-developed with Porsche—a water-cooled V-four Harley. Is it coming, or not?

190

*One of the new middle-class models
mentioned in an earlier chapter,
which did not reach the market thanks
to AMF's restraint. Here is the large
750 cc version, a V-twin with overhead
chain-driven cams. The costly exhaust
tips certainly would have been
rationalized in production.*

Chapter 11

Rulers of the flat track

Top international 250 cc rider Martin Wimmer tells the following tale from the 1985 Grand Prix season, when he, like Freddie Spencer, was competing for the 250 cc world championship, which was won by Spencer along with the 500 cc title. Martin was racing along the ideal line into a decreasing radius turn at the absolute limit of his tires' adhesion, when Spencer, from an impossible position on the outside, slid past him sideways. Not only his rear tire but also the front was pressed flat and drifting away. To Martin it looked like a certain fall, and he tried to stay away from Freddie's most likely line. But Spencer not only came out of the turn faster than Wimmer, but also was able to accelerate his seemingly uncontrollable ride while in the full drift and so gained some distance with this hairy maneuver. Wimmer was impressed.

We Europeans were amazed that American riders were successful from the very start of their late entry into the road racing championship, sanctioned by the FIM, a virtual unknown in the United States, and were often able to win their class title. Pat Hennen, Steve Baker, Kenny Roberts, Freddie Spencer, Eddie Lawson and Randy Mamola are Grand Prix star riders. Their success does not come from the support of Japanese plants seeking identifiable figures to help their advertising in the United States, their most important market. The Americans do not have better works machines or tires at their disposal than their European competitors. Nor do they have a better feel in the seats of their pants.

From the start, professional motorcycle racers in the United States must go through the valuable school of flat- or dirt-track racing. Spread across the entire land, short-, half- or full-mile or TT races take place on weekends or even during the week. In some areas, they are more popular than rodeos or the manifold automobile spectacles. Like the combatants in these events, thousands of dirt-track professionals, often accompanied by wives or mechanics, spend endless hours in their tow vehicles driving from race to race. Many attend ninety or 100 events per year. They live on the hard-won earnings from good placings, more seldom from outright victories. Most motorcycle gypsies run in several classes, fielding a separate machine for each class. Once these have been unloaded, they and their crew can sleep in their Chevy vans. Their diet consists mainly of what's served at such events: hot dogs, burgers and over-sweetened soft drinks.

Except for the TT events, which run over several curves and at least one jump, the races take place on the loose surface of oval tracks, usually still used for horse racing. The surface is stabilized by sprinkling on water and chemicals. Most pilots, as well as spectators, regard the "cushion tracks" as the best. These have loose, clay-rich surfaces which guarantee several pilots on different lines an optimum grip during spectacular drifts.

In the process, these mighty broadslides and extreme drifts churn up the cushion surface after only a few preliminary races. Surface conditions change constantly anyway. If a track is too wet, thanks to rain, condensation or too much added water with too little binder, then drifts as well as acceleration out of the turns are hardly controllable, and many riders lay down in the mud. The dirt spray hinders visibility even more than the dust of the cushion tracks. If track sections dry out during qualifying runs,

then, no later than the finale, there will be hard-fought duels for position, and falls, just before the remaining slippery spots.

If the organizers are too miserly or have too little experience in spraying a dry track, the loose surface of the ideal line will quickly be thrown aside and the underlying dirt will harden. Usually this only happens after several heats. The spinning tires then wear much faster on the hard-polished surface, and discolor it with black or dark blue rubber dust. In the process, the ninety horsepower of each rear wheel cuts ever deeper grooves into the packed clay of the ideal line. This is called a blue groove track.

On the one hand, the heated rubber of this track surface and the hot tires will stick together up to a certain g level; on the other hand, these

The XLR, built from 1957 to 1969, is seen here as an XLRTT of 1958. Displacement was kept at 883 cc, but this racing version of the Sportster was given roller bearings, hot cams, bigger valves and magneto ignition. It was said to give more than 80 horses from 883 cc. One example, exported to England in 1967, *immediately began winning several spectacular races in the 1000 cc class. But because it fit so few racing classes, little effort was expended on its development, and only a few hundred examples were built over the years.*

deep ruts and holes force the riders, sliding around on the treacherous surface, out of their ideal line. Many then try to make good on lost time with drafting duels on the straights and outbraking before the 180 degree turns. Events and championships are decided in favor of those who can best judge the ever-changing conditions and are able to adjust their engines and suspensions accordingly. Because multiple-rider drifts at the end of a race weekend are most difficult to master, they are all the more exciting.

If one stands at the exit of a turn of a mile track, the noise alone overwhelms the observer. The drone of the compact block of approaching bikes on the far straight rings in the ears. They sit up at the entrance to the turn, lean over, and begin ever-increasing skids, before going further

Dick O'Brien, long-time Harley-Davidson racing manager and tuner. First of the men most instrumental in the KR's successes, later the father and developer of the XR 750.

into the turn and approaching the viewer head-on. At that instant, the massive wall of sound hits, made up of the sum total of primeval motors in various load ranges, screaming, grunting and roaring, as well as the howling, screeching and hissing of rolling flattened and slipping tires.

Upright, with overloaded arms gripping the bucking handlebars, forcing the bikes into an even more extreme skidding turn, in the process actually steering with the throttle, they get the last bit of balance from their steel-shod left boots, hopping along the track. Some riders, leaned over even farther and working even harder with arm and foot, with wheels turned full-lock to the outside of the turn, jump ahead by a few positions. Others amaze the viewer by opening the throttle far too early and too hard in the turn, their engines rev freely, their front wheel rises into the air, and they only narrowly avoid a fall. Just before the leaders are released from the centrifugal force of the turn and again reach an upright position, they pull in their arms and legs, their right hands turn the throttles wide open, their left hands are curled around the tube of the front fork to stabilize their mounts, which are swinging from side to side due to the applied power. Now they lean head and shoulders forward and press their chins against the foam rubber pads on their fuel tanks in order to gain some protection against wind and dirt from their number plates. Some try to get into the draft of the man in front, to be pulled along, others try to get out of this position in order to pass. In this way the tightly packed mob on their droning, naked machines flies past, louder and more threatening than an apocalyptic horde.

Among flat trackers, peak power is not cherished; that would only disappear in smoke, and make their ride even more difficult to control. What they need is controllable power to the rear wheels during drifts. The XR motor appears to have exactly the right balance of traction and fat torque curve.

Until recently, the mile races were absolutely dominated by the Harley-Davidson XR 750s. With their four-stroke twins, neither the

Brits nor the Japanese could win so much as a flower pot against the XR competition. A real breakthrough came in 1974 when the incomparable Kenny Roberts rode his monstrous 120 hp Yamaha dirt-track machine with water-cooled 750 cc two-stroke four, derived from the 750 machine used in the world road racing championship.

After efforts as ambitious as they were fruitless, with longitudinally mounted water-cooled 750 cc twins based on their well-known CX motor, Honda brought out an air-cooled V2, derived from their 750 Shadows. When that too failed to achieve the expected breakthrough, Honda bought several fast XRs from private tuners. They were shipped to Japan, measured, studied and copied. Only the Hondas were given four-valve heads. With these devices Honda of America brought the eight-valve back to US tracks and finally won its first Grand National champion title.

Today, Harley-Davidson, too, likes to save on development costs and efforts. Because many riders on half-mile tracks were more successful with light 500 or 600 cc singles than with XRs, especially for TT events, where XRs were becoming too heavy, twenty-five Rotax 500 cc four-strokes were bought in Austria. Mounted in Harley-Davidson frames, these are often entered in TT events.

The first version of the XR 750, derived from the XLR 883, with cast-iron cylinders and heads, lowboy frame and Ceriani fork. During its campaign years,

1969 to 1971, the new Grand National champions were riding English bikes.

Clyde Denzer, here on a 1962 XLCH Sportster, was O'Brien's assistant and second-in-command, and later succeeded him. He had little luck and was soon replaced by Bill Werner, Jay Springsteen's tuner.

Perhaps a whole year's worth of XRs awaiting shipment.

On the mile and half-mile flat tracks, many riders, under certain conditions, deactivated the swing arms by bolting on steel struts. The cast-iron XRs often got noticed due to their overheating problems.

Because of its underwhelming results in previous years, perhaps too because in 1972 the Sportster and Super Glide changed dramatically, the press response to the new XR 750 racers of that year was restrained. It was noted that this was Harley-Davidson's first short-stroker. These new aluminum XRs drew attention in other ways; they took victories in their first races.

Mert Lawwill was multiple Grand National champion in the sixties and early seventies. His assistance in the filming of On Any Sunday helped to create one of the most fascinating motorcycle films ever made. A film crew accompanied him during the entire season.

Mert Lawwill.

Mert Lawwill.

So what harm is there in good motorcycles, high-spirited women, loud rock and roll, and now and then a cool beer? At center, Pulsating Paula, well-known American photographer. Daytona, 1985.

The Harley-Davidson models from Tamiya, in ⅙ scale and with an overall length of about 16 inches, are the greatest. I had tried to customize this 1200 cc Super Glide of 1977 with metallic paint rather than the factory job, but I'm afraid I made a bit of a mess of it. Still, it has a proud place in my bookshelf.

201

Tour Glide rig of 1983, still with the Shovelhead motor, but the new age is coming, with the five-speed transmission and the new frame.

The ten Dragons are younger than their ten Harleys. I'm always impressed how such wild guys keep such antiquated motorcycles alive in hard daily use.

Another epoch at Harley-Davidson ended in 1984, with the special edition of the last Electra Glide with shovelhead motor, four-speed transmission and the old frame.

Here they are, the men responsible for "the look." At left, Willie G. Davidson, company vice president and, among other things, chief designer, along with his design partner Lou Netz, right. Between them, the legendary first 1977 Low Rider, and in front the 1987 Low Rider Custom.

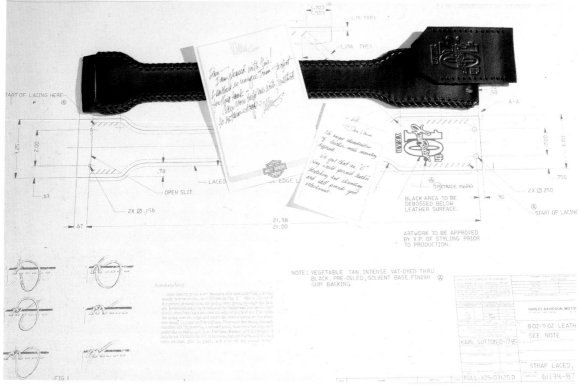

Just a single detail of the special design work done at Harley-Davidson. The tenth anniversary Low Rider Custom was to have a commemorative leather strap between the tank halves; this is how it was worked out.

Just a sample of hundreds of design studies. These hang, clearly visible, in the tiny styling and design studio, so they must have pleased those working there. The principle of the designers is not to produce colorful designs with felt-tip pens on paper, but rather to work them out full scale in three dimensions, and then allow the company brass to decide.

The XL 883 Evolution Sportster of 1987, the entry-level Harley, which the German importer, Harley-Davidson GmbH, also offers in a 27 horse version for those desiring to pay lower road taxes.

No doubt these young ladies will have found the favor of Willie G. (at right) thanks to their classically styled shapes. These are the finalists in the Miss Harley-Davidson (this is, after all, the United States of America) at Harley Heaven, the season opener in Daytona. The presence of the man in the flat cap is its own reward for every visitor. How often has he explained to visitors why there will be no new editions of the Knucklehead or why the current big twin frame looks the way it does?

Softail Custom of 1987, with belt drive, rear disc wheel, 21 inch spoked wheel at the front and special paint. If, in the early years of the Softail, with its hidden shocks, you felt that they might as well have left those off, you'd probably find today's models acceptable.

Softail Heritage 87 in touring trim.

206

Low Rider 87.

In retrospect, I'd like to thank these three posing beauties with the 87 Electra Glide Classic in Morocco. The round trip of over 4,000 miles returned a fuel consumption of better than 45 mpg; one-third to one-half quart of 20W-50 oil was added, the secondary belt was checked a few times, but never tightened, and the bike was cleaned twice. Nothing shook loose and all instruments, lights and radio worked perfectly.

On March 24, 1988, Harley-Davidson's 85th birthday, Willie G. rode into a Harley celebration atop the new Springer Soft Tail FXST-S—and what a birthday present it was! "We're a crazy company," was his first laughing comment. What originally looks like a custom gadget really works wonderfully. Steering seems much easier and exact—maybe this is due to the shortened wheelbase of 64.5 in. down from the regular Soft Tail's 66.3. We rode one of these bikes for nearly a week and every single minute was good fun!

Would Ford bring back tailfins? Of course not. Would Harley repeat its springer front end? You bet they would! Harley was the last important motorcycle company to discontinue springer forks, in 1949. Forty years later, they're the first to bring it back. And how right they are! Problems with wheel shimmy have been overcome with new Teflon-lined bearings replacing the old bronze bearings, technology Harley already uses for its swing arms.

For better cooling, the exhaust ports are at the front, and the mufflers have been relocated. Two 36 mm Mikuni carburetors supply the fuel. The aluminum alloy engines weighed 22 pounds less, despite their larger cooling fins.

Technical drawing of the XRTT.

In road racing, the XRTT looked good against the European competition; its riders could take the BMWs and Italian bikes. It left the vaunted BSA or Triumph three-cylinders far behind, and initially did the same to the four-stroke Japanese competition. But when they learned to make two-stroke, water-cooled four-cylinder machines, and their inherent advantages, the XRTT hadn't a chance. Meanwhile, the street racers experienced a triumphal comeback in the popular BOTT series, the Battle of the Twins, where they engaged in spectacular battles with BMWs and especially the fast Ducatis.

Displacement measurement in the racing department.

210

One of the reasons to look forward to Daytona in March: Gene Church aboard Lucifer's Hammer, the XR BOTT racer sponsored by the HOG (Harley Owners Group). In the past few years, he and Marco Lucchinelli on his Ducati have made the high-priced admission tickets worthwhile. Sometimes one wins, sometimes the other. What's important is what they offer between the start and the finish: super racing!

Although little has changed externally for this 1980 XR 750, the model continues to handle its competitors fairly well.

Springer

Two riders who give away nothing to each other, but give the spectators their money's worth: Scott Parker and Jay Springsteen before and during a race.

The great rivals of the late seventies to early eighties: Jay Springsteen and Randy Goss.

214

Viva Knievel

A totally different top XR rider: Evel Knievel. At one time or another he has done everything, from day laborer to Bible salesman, when he decided to change his life and sell himself to Americans. Added to that, he was a good rider and, if the money was right, a brave man. He could not only add up the money he could make, but also knew how to make it without getting hurt in the process. In the AMF era, he earned a sizeable amount of money through sponsorship from Harley-Davidson. People there will confirm that he did not come cheap, but he honored contracts and appointments and gave the marque a certain media presence by his actions. With increasing propaganda came ever higher fees and ever more dangerous stunts. Time and again, he would beat his own records for jumping over trucks or cars, until he lay it down a few times, hurt himself and reconsidered things. At the time he had a staff of 20, and was still making payments on a Learjet, two custom-made Mack sixteen-wheelers, a headquarters and who knows what else. While injured and unable to ride, he licensed Evel Knievel toys, records, books, movies and did the rounds of schools, chambers of commerce, retirement homes and conventions of pharmacists and lawyers, where he related his version of the American Dream to his captivated listeners. Finally he wanted to jump over the Grand Canyon, which he was not permitted to do, then the Snake River Canyon. Although sponsored by Harley-Davidson and covered with their decals, he preferred a rocket for this jump. TV and all the media were on hand as, shortly after liftoff, the canopy of his Skycycle opened and he bailed out. There followed a long period of silence. The last I've heard about him is that his former press agent turned against him and wrote the "other" book, which Evel didn't like. A fight ensued, and a judge and jury invited Evel to spend some time in jail.

215

Chapter 12

Vaughn Beals, Willie G. and the new Motor Company

Although 1975 was Harley-Davidson's best year ever, with 75,000 units sold, on second glance that number was horrifying. Severe quality control problems appeared in the American-made machines, which cost money not only in warranty claims but also on the production line itself. Half of all the machines sold were the small Italo-Harleys, expensive to produce and ship but sold at rock-bottom prices. The Japanese had already overtaken them in the low- and medium-price ranges, both technically and in price, and the wonderful successes of the two-stroke Italo-Harleys on European racetracks could not disguise that fact. They were really only costing money, and series production was not gaining any new ideas from them. Also, the Italians were as eager to go out on strike as the American workers.

So it came as no surprise that the AMF/ Harley-Davidson cart was soon stuck in the mud. When AMF announced in 1975 that a certain Vaughn Beals would henceforth be president of AMF Harley-Davidson, even the most optimistic observers thought that AMF had hammered yet another nail in the coffin of the last American motorcycle marque. Beals did not appear to be the first choice for this job. Until then, he had never sat on a motorcycle, to say nothing of a Harley. As a business manager, too,

he had not come highly recommended. It must have appeared that AMF boss Rodney Gott couldn't find anyone else as captain for the sinking ship that was Harley-Davidson.

Beals was the son of a Boston accountant, studied aeronautics at MIT, got his master's degree, and worked in the research departments of various companies, until he worked as a development engineer and later director of a string of small high-tech aeronautical establishments. As Harley's new CEO, he soon learned to use his weaknesses as a leader with little experience to his own advantage. In the following years, he strengthened the team spirit in the company's leadership, gave his management colleagues more responsibility, in particular the newly named vice-president and chief designer Willie G. Davidson. He, in turn, used his better position to further his classic designs.

Beals learned to ride motorcycles; judging from the number of cycle trips reported by the media, he must have been enjoying it. He led spectacular excursions of management, for example, from Milwaukee to the opening of Daytona's Bike Week, a distance of several thousand miles, with sealed oil tanks, which proved the quality of the big twins. Or a nationwide Grand Tour, during which they visited most of the listless, frustrated Harley-Davidson dealers. He

216

helped them with actions such as rebates, but also knew how to apply pressure to keep them in line. He departed from AMF's hardline position and initiated a dialog with the labor unions, which began to have a positive influence on quality control and the motorcycles in general. He was enough of a realist to double the size of the engineering department and to give them new avenues to pursue.

The old Harley-Davidson tradition, to be represented in the medium and small classes, was to be resumed. A new, independent line of lightweight Harleys was designed, independent of the old partner Aermacchi. This line grew to the prototype stage. These small to medium Harleys, up to 750 cc, were to have V-twin engines with chain-driven overhead cams, and were to compete in their classes with products from the Big Four Japanese motorcycle makes. The best defense against their importers was considered to be a good offense. Introduction of the new bikes was planned for the early 1980s at the latest. Employees of the engineering department say that they were complete except for minor design details. But production of the small bikes never came to be.

AMF's CEO, Rodney Gott, who had kept Harley on a leash, but a long leash, was replaced by Tom York, who followed a new strategy. He felt that, due to consumers' diminishing buying power, AMF's traditional line of entertainment and recreational products had to be shifted toward more industrial, less crisis-sensitive products. In the AMF conglomerate's most important hobby line, Harley-Davidson, he undertook drastic cuts.

In 1979-1980, York's calculations were not farsighted, but understandable. With about $280 million gross sales, the motorcycle plant showed a net profit of only $12 million. And now, in the face of decreasing motorcycle demand, more than $12 million was to be put into production preparations for the mini-Harleys? No way! Beals therefore resigned as president, but stayed with Harley-Davidson as group executive of AMF Motorcycle.

Under his aegis, the five-speed transmission for the big twin was developed, and the frame redrawn. It was easier to ride, but perhaps did not look as good as the old one. Still, the early market introduction of the five-speed and Tour Glide frame just did not happen. The V2 Evolution big twin line was conceived, which was to replace the honored Shovelhead motors. But at the end of the 1970s, many factors were to stall these projects: the economic recession was setting in.

Meanwhile, the leadership style was again muddled and without direction, and there were again problems with the employees. Harley's

Big toys for big boys. Beals bought the Holiday-Rambler Company in 1986, elevating Harley-David-son to the ranks of upmarket recreation vehicles.

sales figures sank still further, because the quality of the machines being delivered was beneath all contempt. For example, nearly every owner of a 1979 or 1980 big twin had to have the valve seats replaced within the first few thousand miles. The motorcycle industry as well as the general public could only laugh at the unbiased Harley-Davidson reports in motorcycle magazines, with their seemingly endless lists of problems and defects. It's safe to assume that at the

end of the AMF era, the correction of sloppy work detected during the assembly process as well as the endless warranty claims were costing into the tens of millions of dollars. The overhead had to be spread around a smaller number of bikes sold, which meant that prices climbed. At that point, it seemed that the company had lost its only chance for survival.

Any reasonable manager besides Beals would have thrown in the towel, prepared his resume and gone looking for a less aggravating job elsewhere. Not only did Beals stay, but he collected a dozen dissatisfied colleagues from AMF and convinced them to separate from AMF and take over as Harley-Davidson's new management.

AMF was only too glad to finally get rid of Harley, but they didn't want to give it away. The price was set at $75 million. Beals, Willie G., Richard Teerlink and the other managers chipped in $10 million of their own money, and the rest had to be obtained on the open market. The number of rejections gathered by Beals and Teerlink as they went begging for money is an indication of how slim Harley-Davidson's survival chances were seen by the coolly calculating financial community. After endless attempts to borrow $65 million, Citicorp Bank transferred these funds to AMF. The loan was written at 1.5 points above the then-going prime interest rate. The Citicorp financiers got $12 million annually as the reward for their risk.

Under these conditions, an independent Harley-Davidson Motor Company barely would have been able to pay the annual interest on the loan, and eventually would have failed. In the meantime, the new management, in spite of the general decline of the motorcycle market, which had hit Harley worse than most, was able to obtain a better loan from the insurance sector. Fuller utilization of production facilities of nonmotorcycle work further eased the financial burden. Thanks to the low number of motorcycles sold, careful material selection, the relatively high number of people employed as well as the high level of craftsmanship, Harley-Davidson cannot hope to compete in price or marketing with the Japanese, who think in terms of millions of bikes.

Vaughn Beals, long-time Harley-Davidson captain, today admiral of the flotilla.

The introduction of a new generation, regardless of its concept, in the good sales environment of the middle class, would not have been possible without a large investment in production facilities as well as in time and labor. To support the suffering plant, as well as the groaning dealer body, the company was prepared to market motorcycles of character, not as Harleys but rather under their own name, through the Harley-Davidson sales organization.

Some not particularly happy betrothals followed. The attempt to reach an agreement with Moto Morini regarding the US sales of their pretty little Morini 350 and 500 cc V2 motorcycles turned into a disappointment. The widow Morini first made an attractive offer, then did not keep her promises or appointments, and made new demands. Harley-Davidson management lost interest on the not overly enthusiastic courtship for a new Italian bride.

A similar story can be told of deliberations to take over the failed Triumph works in Meriden, England. High demands as well as the realization that even more money would need to be invested in that plant for quality improvement soon drove out these cherished plans of several Harley-Davidson vice-presidents.

Harley engaged Porsche in Weissach, West Germany, to develop a line of liquid-cooled V-engines from a clean sheet of paper to production readiness. The work order called for the following: according to model, the engines were to have 500 to 1200 cc and two, four or six cylinders. Two cams per cylinder bank were planned, yet the powerplants were to outwardly resemble their predecessors. The cost of the project was $10 million.

It couldn't have been done any cheaper in Milwaukee. During the course of the project, American engineers made repeated visits to Weissach. The Porsche engineers could not quite satisfy them. Members of the Harley-Davidson engineering staff recall their disappointment as the clumsy V4 was removed from its shipping crate in Milwaukee. The original hope that it was ready to install turned out to be false. Still, the conditions of the contract as well as the basic characteristics of the engine were attractive, so

Harley and Porsche developed a modern pressed-steel frame to accompany it.

Financing of the remaining development costs of about $20 million, plus the massive sums for the new facilities required for production space and tooling, turned out to be a problem. These were investments that would not show profits for many years. Without new loans or government subsidies, nothing could be done. No favorable terms were to be had from US banks or government offices, so talks with foreign governments in structurally weak areas were initiated. Such a plant would offer about a thousand new jobs, later perhaps more. Talks with the West Berlin Senate and the government of Northern Ireland were extensive but did not lead to a conclusive agreement. According to those responsible at Harley-Davidson, the Nova

Richard F. Teerlink, presently in charge of finance and vice-president of Harley-Davidson's corporate efforts, and also manager of the motorcycle plant.

project was, for the time being, canceled. Whether it will ever be realized is open to speculation; no one will give a definite answer.

If the company is to remain in the luxury motorcycle market, dependent on economic fluctuations, thought must be given to how the plant facilities and employees are to be best utilized and kept secure for a long period. High-paid military contracts were the best way to earn money in the United States during the Reagan era. The Big Spenders, defense secretaries and Pentagon generals, had money to spend. Initially, industry could hardly keep up, but soon adjusted to this secure new market. The realization that defense contracting could bring in fast money was not lost on Beals and Teerlink. Harley, with its well-qualified workers in Milwaukee and York, Pennsylvania, and its experience in industrial processes, was most interested in such government contracts.

Beginning in 1983, plant capacity not fully utilized by motorcycle manufacturing was put to work producing casings for Air Force practice bombs. This and a further subcontract to Beech Aircraft for liquid-fuel rocket engines brought in about $20 million per year. About forty percent of the firm's profits came with a production expenditure of twenty percent.

Protective tariffs against Japanese motorcycles over 700 cc were proposed by the Reagan administration's trade commission and adopted in 1983. This no doubt helped, but the scope is often overrated. The most important reason for these tariffs was the Japanese overproduction and the resulting dumping of these bikes on the American market, as well as the shameless copying of Harley-Davidson design down to the smallest details.

Such import restrictions are only temporarily ordained in the United States, however, and then only after tremendous deliberations, while they have been facts of life in Europe and especially in Japan for decades. A West German customer hands over about a quarter of the price of a Harley not to the importer, but rather to the customs office, to say nothing of other taxes. Yet the German government is relatively restrained when it reaches into our pockets. In Europe, English and Italian authorities collect even more. In West Germany, however, incomprehensible technical requirements add several hundred dollars to the bill. Who, for example, would believe that a Neimann steering lock, easily broken with just one heave, has ever prevented a motorcycle theft?

On the other hand, the Europeans are restrained when compared to the Japanese,

Two of the managers who have been partly responsible for the introduction of better production techniques and the greatly improved new quality control procedures: Dave Gurka and Tom Gelb.

whose tolls effectively prevent importation. In view of this unfair competition, it is not immediately understandable why the Big Four of Japanese motorcycle manufacturing began to howl in pain when the US government finally issued the temporary tariffs.

In 1983, these started at thirty-five percent for the first 7,000 Japanese bikes of each brand (with many times higher total imports) and sank progressively to fifteen percent for the first 15,000 machines of 1986. The numbers would have been 10,000 at ten percent for 1987, but Beals waived the less than overwhelming competitive advantage and asked the US government to lift the protective measures ahead of schedule in 1987.

Chapter 13

A new mousetrap

No other motorcycle marque is represented by so many thirty-, forty-, even fifty-year-old machines. These are not well-preserved veterans visible only at cultural events, but rather bikes still moving with traffic and rewarding the efforts of their proud owners. The reputation built up over generations is one major basis for the indestructible Harley-Davidson legend. No advertising budget could produce anything like this. With all its pride in past achievements, the Harley-Davidson Motor Company could not pay the salaries of its more than 2,500 employees with the proceeds of a legendary past, but only from the sale of today's products.

Helpless in the face of the dominant Japanese competition, by the time of the AMF buyback, Harley-Davidson's leadership had realized that the company would have to undertake drastic changes or disappear as a marque. It wouldn't do any good to complain about the low wages of Japanese laborers, their undemanding mentality, their unfair competitive methods, the mediocre quality and originality as well as their unabashed theft of Harley-Davidson designs. An increasing number of customers were buying Japanese bikes, and ever fewer found their way to the exclusive Harley-Davidson market niche. If the fate of the British marques or the Indian

was to be avoided, it would be necessary to take a good, hard look at the company. For the huge Japanese cycle manufacturers were not selling their products year after year without profit, nor under their own costs, but rather achieved their low prices by approaching production and marketing in a more reasonable manner—and because they were not afraid to learn and, in the process, be laughed at.

Whether you liked their motorcycles or not, the management of the Big Four Japanese bike makers didn't give much cause for amusement. To the contrary, the Japanese considered the Milwaukee factory a better, or sometimes worse, but generally a force equal to their own, and rightfully so. The Americans knew little of the effective Japanese Kanban methods, a warehousing system that offered tremendous cost savings and quality control improvements. Or of the just-in-time delivery of parts to the assembly line. The new Harley-Davidson management now had to stay after school to learn these. Vaughn Beals, Willie G. Davidson, Clyde Fessler, Kurt Woerpel, Tom Gelb and others forgot the slogan that many bikers wore on their T-shirts, We don't care how they do it in Japan, and analyzed the methods of Japanese car and bike manufacturers.

They were impressed. It was not robots, modern electronics or a quicker pace that gave them the lead in production. The real difference was the more efficient organization of employees and machines. The workers carry out their greater responsibilities and contribute more to the well-being of the company. The machines are adapted to new setups more quickly and are used more efficiently.

After considering this for a while, Harley-Davidson sent middle-management executives to seminars in Statistic Process Control at universities. Their new knowledge was passed on through internal courses at the plant. Workers needed to take part in these and diverse experiments for a total of only about fifteen hours, foremen and managers about ninety hours. The result was the independent MAN system—Material As Needed—which constituted more than another Kanban application.

With MAN, every part appears only where and when it is needed in the assembly process.

To make it work, outside suppliers and the company's own warehousing, accessory and manufacturing departments had to be included in the program and coordinated. This was not easy, as parts came from all over the world; the cast wheels came from Australia, the carburetors from Japan, the pistons from West Germany, to name a few. Many at Harley-Davidson thought the whole thing was a passing management fad; acceptance on the shop floor took a while.

The basic idea was that no longer would a high number of a single model be produced exclusively over the course of many weeks or months. Now Harley would produce the bikes required by current market demand. Before, the conversion of the machinery from one model to the next had taken days or even weeks. Now, for example, the dies for the hydraulic presses were stored next to the presses themselves, where before they had been brought out of a storage shed by forklift. The setup times of even the

The Capitol Drive plant, also known as the Butler plant, in the Milwaukee suburb of Wauwatosa. In the next few pages we will look at engine and trans- *mission manufacturing, which is presently performed in this facility.*

223

The Tillitron Gear Coder. Here, the gears and camshafts of the Sportster and FLH are precisely measured and mated in the best fitting combinations. Batches of 14 such sets are marked and sent on to assembly.

The Cincinnati T-10 unit. It machines the rough crankshaft halves of the XL line.

This CNC mill machines the blanks for the five-speed transmission.

This automatic line pushes steel bars through six CNC lathes, two saws and one grinding process, and puts out blanks for gears in the five-speed transmission.

This worker is checking the bores and valve seats of an Evolution cylinder head. The results are entered in the Statistical Operator Control (SOC) list at right. If the parts are getting too close to the tolerance limits, he can immediately look for the source of the problem.

The SOC lists are part of most work stations at the Capitol Drive plant. Because SOC lets errors be recognized immediately, and results in tighter tolerances, manufacturing costs drop while quality improves.

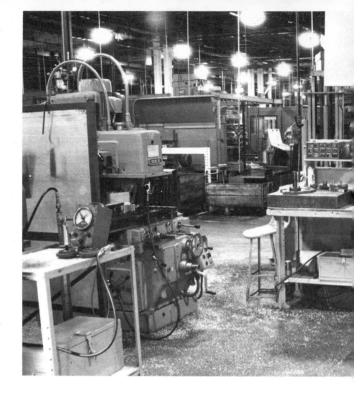

Outsourced parts such as the FL crankcase or the German pistons are checked before being released to production. This specialist is applying his micrometer to the crankshaft bearing bore.

smallest machines were reduced to just a fraction of their previous times.

The warehousing costs of the material and parts required for production, as well as that of finished, unshipped motorcycles, fell by over $10 million per year. Because production and delivery were on an as-needed basis, the motorcycles were protected for their short stay in the warehouse; delicate parts of the vehicle were protected by foam pads.

During my plant visit, I was pleased that work progressed quietly, apparently with concentration and without pressure. For an engine and transmission factory, it appeared extraordinarily clean, quiet and roomy. The generous space resulted from the elimination of unneeded warehouse space. The low noise level was explained by the large number of new machines, many encapsulated or sound insulated to keep the racket down. Dirt, too, was reduced as a result. Furthermore, all manufacturing steps for a single component were no longer spread out, but rather concentrated in production cells. Also, housecleaning was performed more frequently, to keep thick air, filthy floors or general dust and dirt from spoiling the general mood on the shop floor.

Those working in certain teams are voluntarily part of so-called Quality Circles; they attend courses to better their understanding of materials and manufacturing steps, and impose increasingly tighter tolerances on themselves. This employee involvement has extended over several years. Many normal management meetings have since been open; all employees are not only invited to attend, but also take part in the

One of the enclosed dynamometer cells, in which the completed Evolution engine is checked for power output, noise, tightness and appearance.

SOC is also applied to the manufacture of the big twin oil pumps. Whenever possible, manufacture and finishing of a part are combined in one enclosed cell, to permit close communication between those involved. This worker is drilling close-tolerance holes.

The heat treatment department, with nitriding ovens, draft ovens, induction hardening and annealing machines. These expensive processes were kept in-house to maintain quality, although outside firms had made attractive offers.

Every assembled transmission is checked for easy shifting, noise and tightness.

Every day, a motor is chosen at random from the assembly line. It is then run on this dyno under varying loads for several hours, and is then disassembled. In the process, factors such as correct assembly, possible damage or fastener tightening torques are checked. If deviations appear, they are pointed out to the machine operator, who is responsible for their elimination.

The computer-controlled Cincinnati Milacron Cinturn lathe is at the beginning of the crankshaft manufacturing process. It is loaded and unloaded by an attached robot arm.

discussions. A Job Security Committee, composed of management and employee representatives, meets regularly.

Harley Hotline, the small plant newspaper, a flyer really, is encouraged to be irreverent and critical. In it, for example, legal boss Tim Hoelter is asked to try to make his presentations less boring. Willie G.'s son Bill Davidson, who works in administration, had his not always masterful social graces presented in the form of a Lotus 1-2-3 program. The general manager of the Butler plant, Dick Davidson, is often taken to task for his occasional rudeness and lack of participation in sporting activities. Racing manager

The combined final assembly line for big twin engine and transmission as well as for the Sportster powerplant, moving at an agreeable pace. Thanks to the MAN (Material As Needed) warehousing and inventory control, the assembly process works flawlessly, without parts pileups or gaps.

Bill Werner, too, is implored to lose ten pounds or so.

Sporting activities to promote good health are encouraged. Points are distributed for running, cycling or swimming achievements, points that can be exchanged for gifts. Other health programs are also sponsored. Even older employees are proud to show their affiliation with the company by wearing their Harley T-shirts.

Now, managers don't stay managers because they're nice and friendly, but rather because they can do their arithmetic. The bottom line for the company is promising. Warehousing has saved the company $30 to $40 million. The new, higher-quality standards, which result in fewer rejects, rework or warranty claims, have saved at least as much and have won over new customers. The enormously reduced machinery conversion time has markedly increased production. The inclusion of the employees is noticed in many ways, not only by the many black T-shirts in the plant. And sick days were cut in half, absenteeism by forty-four percent.

The Harley-Davidson fiberglass plant is located about 150 miles from Milwaukee, in Tomahawk, Wisconsin. Harley bought this boat factory in order to become independent of unsatisfactory outside suppliers, there to build its own full-dresser parts, among other things. Beginning in 1969, saddlebags and fairings were delivered from here. Despite the experienced personnel, it took a while before things like material-specific shrinkage were mastered, because the boat hulls made previously did not need to be made to such high standards of accuracy. Another problem was applying similar paint to both the metal and fiberglass parts of a bike. That's why bags and fairings were delivered in white until the mid-seventies. As can be seen at any dealership, today's paint quality and regularity are the best in the business.

Chapter 14

Evolution

In the spring of 1987, Beals requested an early lifting of the protective tariffs because, with the Evolution models, Harley-Davidson was offering an outstanding motorcycle generation which regained lost territory. Despite theoretical design disadvantages, such as the pushrod engine (no longer considered modern practice), the separate transmission and generous use of materials (they were no longer bound to keeping the parts count low), the buyer can hardly find a more comfortable and more pleasant large touring machine—to say nothing of the level of style and presence of the production custom bikes. Sales figures reached the (reduced) magic level of 30,000 which marked the break-even point between profit and loss.

The ways in which the Evolution Harleys were accepted by motorcycle enthusiasts lifted the spirits of not only the managers; every Harley-Davidson employee and dealer felt encouraged. After many years of losses, up to $20 million per year, the Harley-Davidson plant, long given up for dead, seemed to regain its footing after its long crisis and to take a new perspective. Despite declining sales in the motorcycle market as a whole, Milwaukee increased its output from year to year. And finally, the balance sheets for 1984, 1985 and 1986 each showed a $10 million profit.

In 1985 the manufacturing rights for sporting trikes were obtained, but the investment for a Tri-Glide was simply too high, and its sales potential too low.

The dramatic changes at Harley-Davidson did not go unnoticed. On July 8, 1986, Beals rode a 1986 Super Glide, resplendent in special "liberty" paint scheme, down Wall Street and into the halls of the New York Stock Exchange. There he announced the issue of two million shares of Harley-Davidson preferred stock, with a value of $10 million, and non-voting stock in the amount of $70 million. These stocks are truly not rockets, but their development since then has been positive and prices are presently between $20 and $30 per share. The biker magazine *Easyriders* presents these stock prices in a monthly column.

In light of the no-holds-barred competition on Wall Street today, the Harley-Davidson articles of incorporation have a few built-in preventative measures to avoid the possibility of a hostile takeover. Now better supplied with capital thanks to the general trend of the market, a desire to secure the company by acquiring profit centers removed from the motorcycle industry was met by the purchase, at the end of 1986, of Holiday-Rambler, a high-profile manufacturer of motorhomes. The price was $35 million in cash and $120 million in credit. For those who may be interested in the current prices of these RVs, Holiday Ramblers are priced between $10,000 and $180,000.

The new Evolution motors, designed with great ambition, built with the highest attention to detail and presented with pride, had a few initial flaws. Inside the alloy motors, the pistons moved within liners of cast iron. This is for a well-known reason; cast-iron liners and aluminum pistons adjust to one another better than if

Its history goes back to 1978. Warranty and service problems with the Shovels caused the engineers to rethink its design. Higher reliability, increased torque and more power with lower production costs were demanded. The first prototypes were finished in the same year, concept and basic specifications in 1979. In 1980, frame height and motor mounts on several current motorcycle models were modified in preparation for the expected new arrival. A small batch of test machines ran off over 250,000 test miles and 5,600 dyno hours before the Evolution V2 was considered ready for delivery to dealers in 1984. Originally they planned to present the motor in 1983, but it was decided to spend the extra time getting rid of a few more bugs.

both were made of aluminum. In the new motor's first year, one or more lathes which turned the liners had a hidden defect in the chucking mechanism. With tight tolerances between piston and cylinder wall, these liners, once installed, sold and ridden, caused piston seizures and warranty claims due to their unseen oval shape. The Capitol Drive troubleshooting team finally found the cause.

Because the plant had released other brand-name 20W-50 oils to supplement the Harley-Davidson oils for the Evolution engines, many customers thought that they could save a few pennies by using non-Harley oils in other locations throughout their bikes. These miserly riders soon were punished by unstoppable bucking from Harley-Davidson's first oil-bath clutches. They then overloaded both dealerships and the plant with warranty claims. At the plant, technical detectives determined that the clutch grabbing only occurred when the owners had violated Harley's express requirement to use only the proper Harley-Davidson oil in this location.

As soon as "foreign" oils were introduced to the clutch, it began to alternately grab and slip, and it could not be broken of this habit, even if it was replaced by the proper Harley fluid. The clutch was redesigned to make the clutch less demanding, and Harley absorbed part or all of the cost of required repairs. Further, within the first year, a strange, unpleasant rattle from within the cylinder head surprised many riders: broken valve springs. This was traced to a material problem of a small proportion of all valves manufactured and was soon corrected.

Such occasional difficulties should not confuse our vision. Those who have had the opportunity to ride the new Harleys every now and then, as I have, have little doubt that they are the most beautiful, most stylish and highest quality motorcycles on our tiny planet. Apparently, the new Motor Company has made the grade. Now if only the quality would remain while the price dropped a little . . .

For a suggested retail price of nearly $12,000 for an Electra Glide, you can buy a decent middle-class sedan. If this amount is

The FXEF, Super Glide Fat Bob, with its only slightly modified Shovel frame, was basically a Super Glide brought into the Evolution era, and, like the earlier Super Glide, remained the entry-level big Harley.

The Low Rider FXSB of 1983 was propelled by the new motor and the double belt drive of the Sturgis. In this way, the Low Rider reunited several bike lines. This is the FXSB of 1985.

3 AND 1/16 inches

Since 1984, the FXWG Wide Glide has definitely not been Harley's most extreme chopper. Here, the 1985 model.

invested in a motorcycle, you should expect a great deal. In the case of the long-distance big twin, the buyer gets a fair amount of equipment, workmanship, classic design, marque image, prestige and the promise of great experiences to come. Whether or not the price-to-benefit ratio is acceptable must be decided by the individual.

Those who feel that a massive 1340 cc two-cylinder pushrod engine is antiquated have never ridden a V2 Evolution bike. Full power from the lowest revs, the possible disdain for shifting but with the availability of a broad, useful rev range, the maintenance-free belt drive as well as the long-range fuel economy are important points. At least for me, it was pleasure without regrets to be allowed to ride new press bikes.

With enough effort, other Harleys will offer much the same; I have always said so in this book. Naturally, the Blockhead has more power with less roughness, and is less sensitive. If the power is used, there is less need to fear the eventual waiting by the side of the road for emergency service. That's why, of all the equipment on the big twin tourer, I would like to further sing the praises of the sound system. I had the opportunity to try a 1987 Electra Glide Classic press machine in late November 1986, and used this fine opportunity to take a three-week journey through Spain and Morocco. Naturally I noted the stereo and speakers in the fairing, but never realized their potential. My thoughts were more on whether the passes were free of snow, my warm clothes and rain gear. Never in my wildest dreams did I think of stocking up on audio cassettes.

We had good luck with the weather. It rained off and on, and we were not spared fog, but south of Lyon, France, the sun shone with increasing warmth. And from there onward, relaxed and comfortable, I played with the radio. At our normal cruising speed of 70 mph, this was super! Now the stations there broadcast in French, which I don't even begin to understand, and I still don't like disco. So I began buying one or two cassettes at every fuel or rest stop. Talking Heads, Verdi arias by Pavarotti, Beethoven symphonies, Tina Turner, Siouxsie and the Banshees, a sort of random walk through several different musical disciplines. Some nuances even reached the ears of my passenger. Surrounded by music and riding through a wonderful landscape—I had never covered the long haul to and from my mother's vacation home in Malaga, Spain, so pleasantly.

No one can tell me that such a device is not necessary. In my opinion, it's a luxury, but one to which you gladly get accustomed. This gadget, which is standard equipment on all touring bikes since 1987, represents the optimum in the field of motorcycle surround sound. It is only necessary to lay your hand on the radio to turn it on, insert cassettes and to set the automatic rpm and gear-dependent sound level adjustment before departing.

During the trip, switching from AM to FM, automatic traffic report decoder, search/scan, and switching between radio and cassette, auto-reverse, and for the next selection on the cassette and manual volume control, are accomplished by pressing buttons underneath the turn indicator buttons on the grips. The device has three bands, twenty watts per channel, Dolby, Dynamic Noise Reduction, bass and treble adjustments, a digital display that is readable both in sunlight and at night, and is waterproof. If this is still not enough, an intercom system and CB radio can be added.

So those who have done without a great touring Harley because they would forego their beloved sounds while cruising can now listen, relaxed and without being obvious, with the volume set at the proper level whether moving at 80 mph or at stoplights, thanks to the automatic volume control.

The acoustics of the engine can just as well be enjoyed without musical accompaniment. It is the unmistakable sound of a Harley big twin. The V2 ohv concept, begun with the Knucklehead and developed over the years with the Pan and Shovelhead, had its character and load capacity refined through forty years of development. The philosophy of the first ohv twin is hardly different from that of the current generation, but the everyday reliability of the modern machine is vastly improved. The big-displace-

Although the 1986 Wide Glide, with its classic frame and metallic flame design, recalled its mighty origins, it had been dethroned by the astoundingly logical Softail.

The front part of the FXST Softail is unmistakably derived from the Wide Glide. But the seating—incredible! Low, very low, with our long-absent friend, the horseshoe oil tank, missing for over a decade. What at first glance appears to be a rigid frame is in reality a rear swing arm, whose gas pressure shock is horizontally mounted between the lower frame tubes. This is the 1985 model.

Softail FXST of 1986. Engine and such of this primeval machine are not mounted in rubber, but rather are allowed to shake the rider without constraint, presumably to point out that the FXST is a real motorcycle—of which there can be no doubt.

The Custom Softail FXST-C of 1986. Aluminum disc rear wheel, sissy bar, two-tone paint job, partly blackened, partly chromed and partly polished motor. I was able to ride the Softail as well as the new FXST-C for several hundred kilometers and was almost more impressed by the suspension than by its appearance.

It just had to happen. The design surprise of the year 1986, the FLST Softail Heritage 86—from the FXST chopper back the other way to the tourer. To quote Willie G.: "This classic style has belonged to us for decades. We have developed its function and have never abandoned it. We are not repeating it, but rather combine it with our present technology."

And one year later they combined it in the FLST-S, Softail Heritage Special, with not-so-functional bombast as the fringed bags, mounted too far back, and conchos on the saddle. The police windscreen and blue and cream paint work match these well.

The FLT of 1985 was the first Harley with which I felt comfortable for hours on end at 95 to 100 mph on the Autobahn, although I remained well clear of the redline. I was none the worse, nothing fell off on the way, brakes and suspension went along with all this, and fuel and oil consumption were within acceptable limits.

ment Shovel as well as the Blockhead retain the same bore and stroke dimensions of 3.50×4.25 in., as well as the same crankcase and crankshaft. Displacement stayed at 1340 cc, power increased about ten percent and the fatter torque curve peaks at lower rpm.

Compression was increased to a still civil level of 8.5:1. Depending on model, the traditional separate but firmly coupled transmission with four or five speeds is installed. Both cylinders are interchangeable. The cylinder included angle is, as always, forty-five degrees. Piston, connecting rods, lifters and cams are new. The pistons are barrel-shaped, ground on two axes, to reduce friction with the cylinder walls. They are now flatter and shorter, made of aluminum with twelve percent silicon. The hollow push-

rods force oil into the cylinder heads, replacing the separate lines. As a result, lubricants no longer build up in the valve guides, and don't flow into the combustion chambers, but rather run back into the crankcase. Oil consumption dropped to nearly unbelievable levels.

For ease in servicing, the rocker boxes are built up from three parts. The rockers are lighter and, like tappets, camshaft, pushrods and pistons, are made of better materials and finished better. Valve duration is decreased. The valves are asymmetrically mounted, inlet twenty-seven degrees and outlet thirty-one degrees to the centerline. The valves are smaller, thereby able to reach farther into the chamber. The straighter inlet passages have a smaller diameter. The redesigned combustion chamber as well as the

Still, when it came to the layout for engine, suspension and other components of the grand touring machines, the unanimous opinion in Milwaukee was that the rider should feel how fast he was going. The designers did not feel that stress-free riding at 140 mph was a worthwhile goal, a senseless and foolish aberration. That is why the Harley-Davidson touring machines develop relatively little power by today's distorted standards, and therefore provide pleasure with their overall well-balanced riding characteristics. Here is the new FLHT Electra Glide of 1985, based on the FLT. In that year, the FLT and FLHT still had the heavy air filter mounted on the carburetor.

Grand Touring Edition of the Sport Glide, FXRD, of 1987. As has been said of its Shovel precursors, it's missing flair or flavor despite its good characteristics. It is a little of what no Harley should ever be: boring. On the market, it appears a bit contrived. Bags and seating are not as roomy as on the bigger bikes and the radio in the fairing is underwhelming. This isn't a Japanese bike, but why does it look like one?

WOULD YOU SELL
AN UNRELIABLE MOTORCYCLE
TO THESE GUYS?

Add all the accessories from the Harley-Davidson catalog to the Electra and Tour Glide classics and you receive the Ultra-Glide. Introduced in 1989, the Ultra should bring some Gold Wing riders back home. The Ultra includes removable fairing lowers with gloveboxes, vent deflectors, cruise control and cigarette lighter; the additional rear speakers also have a separate 40 watt amp of their own. With the CB and intercom, the customer may choose between the hand-held CB mic or a helmet speaker system mic as standard equipment. All this and the bike weighs in at only 765 lb. Except for the Sportster line, all Harleys now have belt drive. No power loss, no reaction to load reversal, no lubrication and little tightening, yet much lighter than a driveshaft. Well, given that, I know what I could choose.

FLHS Electra Glide Sport. Not everyone wants a stereo in the fairing; for that, there's the living room. A police windshield is known to reflect less motor noise and is (ahem) more wind-cheating. But the roomy-looking saddlebags are too small for a real tour. Their inner walls are deformed by the rear shocks and oil tank.

modified spark plug location provide faster flame propagation with lower flame temperatures.

To make a long story short, one of the best reasons to be interested in a new Harley is the incredible Blockhead motor.

Me, November 1986, with the Electra Glide Classic on the Rock of Gibraltar, between two examples of metalwork from different centuries.

The future and the past combine in Harley's latest Springer. With all their knowledge, computer-backed design and advanced construction potential, Mark Tuttle and the other designers at Harley have taken a step backward to the classic front end. The new springer has a full four inches of suspension travel compared with the old layout's two inches. The bearings are made of Teflon and are extremely durable. Easier steering and better suspension are the results; the looks are thrown in as an extra.

240

Postscript

There is no single author who, in his Harley-Davidson works, has not made numerous, often insidious errors. What single person has been at the scene of every part of Harley-Davidson's eighty-year history? Time and again, a collector would show me a Harley whose specification and serial number clearly indicated its year of birth, but which, according to research by colleagues, should have ceased production years earlier. I have ridden wonderful 500 cc machines that should not even exist. Many facts, seen as established history, can be traced back through seven books and perhaps twenty magazine articles of the last thirty or fifty years to their first appearance as erroneous reports.

Bibliography and sources

Before beginning the actual writing chores, I prepared material for this picture book by getting enlightening insights and bloodshot eyes in the following cellars, offices and living rooms.

Harley-Davidson's archives and public relations department

Harley-Davidson GmbH press department

Harrah's automobile collection archives

The Austrian Motorcycle Archive, Dr. Helmut Krackowizer

Joachim von Barnekow collection

Bud Ekins collection

Mike Parti collection

Mike Shundo collection

Carlo Heller collection

Uwe Illger collection

Christian Timmermann collection

And finally the ring binder, paper piles and Ikea bookshelves belonging to Christel and me.

As much as possible, I have gotten my data from company documents or contemporary publications. Of those Harley-Davidson publications I have used the following:

The Enthusiast

The Mounted Police Officer

Sales, promotional and press material

Owners handbooks

Repair manuals

H-D service tips

Shop Dope

Parts and accessory lists

Pacific Motorcycling

Western Motorcyclist

Motorcycling

Motorcycle Illustrated

Motorcycling & Bicycling

Motor Cycling

Publications of the Antique Motorcycle Club of America

Easyriders

Hot Bike

Supercycle

Cycle
Cycle Guide
Cycle World
Walneck's Old Time Cycles
Motorrad

Peter "Haunsi" Wolf
Uwe Illger
M. Schrumpf
Motorpresse archives
Christel Holst and Wolfgang Wiesner

Photo acknowledgments

Harley-Davidson Motor Company, Inc.
Harley-Davidson GmbH
Hans Weschta
Dr. Helmut Krackowizer
Gerhard and Hans von Bigtwin
Arthur Schrödinger

Final thanks

In looking through archives, in photography, copying, sorting, assembling, correcting, maintaining contacts and so on, this woman was again very important and helped me to avoid missing deadline by even greater margins: Christel Holst.

Index